STUDENT STUDY GUIDE
CRIMINAL JUSTICE
MAINSTREAM AND CROSSCURRENTS

JOHN RANDOLPH FULLER, PH.D.
State University of West Georgia

Upper Saddle River, New Jersey 07458

Executive Editor: Frank Mortimer, Jr.
Associate Editor: Sarah Holle
Production Editor: Barbara Cappuccio
Director of Manufacturing and Production: Bruce Johnson
Managing Editor: Mary Carnis
Manufacturing Buyer: Cathleen Petersen
Cover Image: Getty Images

Copyright © 2006 by Pearson Education, Inc., Upper Saddle River, New Jersey, 07458.
Pearson Prentice Hall. All rights reserved. Printed in the United States of America. This publication is protected by Copyright and permission should be obtained from the publisher prior to any prohibited reproduction, storage in a retrieval system, or transmission in any form or by any means, electronic, mechanical, photocopying, recording, or likewise. For information regarding permission(s), write to: Rights and Permissions Department.

Pearson Prentice Hall™ is a trademark of Pearson Education, Inc.
Pearson® is a registered trademark of Pearson plc
Prentice Hall® is a registered trademark of Pearson Education, Inc.

Pearson Education LTD.
Pearson Education Singapore, Pte. Ltd
Pearson Education, Canada, Ltd
Pearson Education–Japan
Pearson Education Australia PTY, Limited
Pearson Education North Asia Ltd
Pearson Educación de Mexico, S.A. de C.V.
Pearson Education Malaysia, Pte. Ltd

10 9 8 7 6 5 4 3 2 1
ISBN 0-13-112282-7

Contents

Study Guide Orientation v

Part One	**Crime: Problems, Measurement, Theories, and Law**	
Chapter 1	The Problem of Social Control	1
Chapter 2	The Nature and Measurement of Crime	18
Chapter 3	Theories of Crime	32
Chapter 4	Criminal Law	47
Part One	Match the Case	62
Part Two	**Enforcing the Law**	
Chapter 5	History and Organization of Law Enforcement	63
Chapter 6	Controlling the Police	77
Chapter 7	Issues in Policing	92
Part Two	Match the Case	104
Part Three	**Role of the Courts**	
Chapter 8	History and Organization of Courts	105
Chapter 9	Working in the Courtroom	120
Chapter 10	The Disposition: Plea Bargaining, Trial, and Sentencing	134
Part Three	Match the Case	148
Part Four	**From Penology to Corrections and Back**	
Chapter 11	History of Control	149
Chapter 12	The Contemporary Prison	161
Chapter 13	Corrections in the Community	173
Part Four	Match the Case	185
Part Five	**Problems in the Crosscurrents**	
Chapter 14	Juvenile Delinquency and Juvenile Justice	186
Chapter 15	Crime and Values: Drugs, Gambling, and Sex Work	200
Chapter 16	Present and Emerging Trends: The Future of Criminal Justice	213
Part Five	Match the Case	225
Appendix A	Answers to Even-Numbered Study Guide Questions	226

Study Guide Orientation

Welcome to the study guide for *Criminal Justice: Mainstream and Crosscurrents*. Use it to prepare for tests, quizzes, essays, and to get to know the material really well. Exactly how well will depend on how often and how rigorously you use it. This study guide provides many different ways for you to approach the material and highlights the main issues in the book from several perspectives. Students who work diligently through the study guide can expect to master the material at a greater rate than those who don't. Here are the exercises:

Learning Objectives
This is a list of what you should know after reading the chapter.

Chapter Summary and Key Concepts
This outline delineates each chapter's most important concepts.

Key Terms
The key terms are also defined in the textbook's margins and noted at the end of each chapter with their page numbers.

Short Answer Questions
Short answer questions are much like the essay questions that you would find on a test. This is a good chance to practice your critical thinking skills and grasp important concepts.

Study Guide Questions
The study guide questions consist of multiple choice, true/false, and fill-in-the-blank, just like you would find on a test. These will especially help you learn and remember important terms and court cases.

Find a Flash
Each chapter has one or more news flash features that cover real-life events in the criminal justice system. Use the Find a Flash exercise to discover and analyze the workings of the criminal justice system. This feature is especially useful for learning how the media treats criminal justice issues.

What Agency Am I?
Get to know your federal criminal justice agencies here. This is an especially good exercise for those who wish to become criminal justice professionals.

Word Search
This is not your average Sunday paper word search. To get the words you have to search for, first you have to fill in the blanks of the definitions. This is a pretty good vocabulary builder. Hint: The search words are not always key terms.

Match the Case
There are five of these exercises, one for each part of the book. Each exercise uses all the cases from the Case in Point features in that part. For example, Match the Case: Part One features all

the Case in Point cases from Part One. All you have to do is draw a line from the case to its point.

Advice on Studying and Reading
My advice on studying is that there really isn't any. Each student has his or her own best way to study, so do what works best for you. What's important is finding what works best for you and doing it regularly. Some people study best in low-noise places, like coffee shops, while others prefer small groups at the library, while others study best if they are completely alone. Some people actually study best by cramming. You may or may not be one of them. Regardless of how you like to study, this study guide will be a great help. Also, reviewing your notes immediately after class is a good thing to do, as is reading your textbook.

While the criminal justice system is a rich mine for television and film, these two mediums don't do it justice (so to speak). The U.S. criminal justice system is far more surprising, disturbing, interesting, and amazing than most people realize, and *Criminal Justice: Mainstream and Crosscurrents* gives you the best look at how and why it works the way it does. We hope this study guide will help you get the most out of your textbook.

Have fun!

Chapter 1
The Problem of Social Control

Learning Objectives
After reading this chapter, you should be able to:
1. Appreciate the level and quality of the information concerning ideas about the criminal justice system.
2. Understand how the criminal justice system works with other institutions to control the behavior of individuals.
3. Look at the criminal justice system and ask whether the system metaphor is illustrative or misleading.
4. Discuss the picture of crime presented by the media and suggest ways in which it might be improved.
5. Explain how the number of cases decreases as we trace their movement through the criminal justice system.
6. List and discuss the multiple goals of the criminal justice system.
7. Explain why the criminal justice system is the system of last resort.

Chapter Summary and Key Concepts
Chapter 1 introduces the challenges of social control, the definition of crime, and the U.S. criminal justice system.

The U.S. Criminal Justice System
- The criminal justice system is the institution of last resort.
- The criminal justice system must respond in the name of society when crimes are committed.
- The criminal justice system protects individual rights as a part of the law enforcement function.
- The criminal justice system must balance the imposition of order and the preservation of individual rights.
- The criminal justice system may be envisioned as a funnel that includes crimes, crimes known to the police, investigation, arrests, booking, charges filed by the prosecutor, the grand jury, initial appearance, preliminary hearing, arraignment, bail, plea bargaining, trial, sentencing, probation, appeal, prison, parole, and, in a few cases, capital punishment.
- The criminal justice system has multiple goals, including deterrence, incapacitation, retribution, rehabilitation, and restoration.
- Other means of social control besides the criminal justice system include the family, religion, schools, and the media.

Crime
- Crime can be described as an action that violates the rules of society to the point of harming citizens or the society itself. Other crimes, such as espionage crimes, threaten a society's political stability.

- Crime may go undetected, and the harm is not generally perceived.
- Broad categories of crime include sensationalized crime, street crime, corporate crime, white-collar crime, and organized crime.
- Sensationalized crimes are given such vast resources that they distort the public's perception of the amount and seriousness of crime.
- Corporate crime involves the breaking of laws by a company's employees in pursuit of profit. White-collar crime usually involves employees harming a corporation.
- The actual crime rate does not always accurately reflect the public's perception of the crime rate.
- Officials use discretion to decide which cases proceed further into the criminal justice system and which ones do not. Many of the crimes that do enter the system also may be eventually excluded.
- Many crimes that enter the system are systematically excluded for a variety of reasons, including cost, discretion, and errors.

Law Enforcement
- Law enforcement tasks, along with courts and corrections tasks, are divided differently across the local, state, and federal branches of government.
- Most law-enforcement authority lies at the local level.
- State law enforcement functions usually are confined to specialized missions such as highway patrol and bureaus of investigation.
- Federal law enforcement functions include a wide range of agencies that enforce federal laws and assist state and local governments.
- Federal law enforcement includes the Border Patrol, the U.S. Citizenship and Immigration Service (formerly the Immigration and Naturalization Service), the United States Marshals, the U.S. Customs Service, the Drug Enforcement Administration (DEA), and the Bureau of Alcohol, Tobacco, Firearms, and Explosives (ATF).

Key Terms

arraignment
A court appearance in which the defendant is formally charged with a crime and asked to respond by pleading guilty, not guilty, or *nolo contendere*.

bailiff
An officer of the court responsible for executing writs and processes, making arrests, and keeping order in the court.

bill of indictment
A declaration of the charges against an accused person that is presented to a grand jury to determine whether enough evidence exists for an indictment.

Bureau of Alcohol, Tobacco, Firearms, and Explosives
A law enforcement organization that enforces federal laws and regulations relating to alcohol, tobacco, firearms, explosives, and arson.

chemical castration
Anti-androgen drugs, usually administered by injection, that have the effect of lowering the testosterone level and blunting the sex drive in males.

clearance rates
The number of crimes that have been solved by the police. Often, offenders who are arrested for a crime will give information about other crimes they have committed. This allows police to "clear" those cases.

county stockade
A component of a county corrections system. The stockade usually holds offenders who have already been sentenced. Because of overcrowding in state systems, many county stockades hold state felony offenders on a contract basis.

discretion
The power of a judge, public official, or law enforcement officer to make decisions on issues within legal guidelines. For example, a prosecutor exercises discretion about which cases are inserted into the criminal justice system.

Drug Enforcement Administration
Enforces U.S. controlled substances laws and regulations. Also brings to the U.S. criminal system organizations involved in the growing, manufacture, and/or distribution of controlled substances to be trafficked in the United States.

electronic monitoring
A form of intermediate punishment in which an offender is allowed to remain in the community but must wear an electronic device that allows the authorities to monitor his or her whereabouts. Electronic monitoring may also be done via telephone.

Federal Bureau of Investigation
The principal investigative arm of the Department of Justice. It investigates the crimes assigned to it and provides cooperative services to other law enforcement agencies.

felony
A crime punishable by a term in state or federal prison and sometimes by death. In some instances, a sentence for a felony conviction may be less than one year. Felonies are sometimes called "high crimes."

Immigration and Naturalization Service
An agency of the Department of Justice responsible for enforcing the laws regulating the admission of foreigners to the United States and for administering immigration benefits, including the naturalization of applicants for U.S. citizenship.

misdemeanor
A crime considered less serious than a felony. Usually tried in the lowest local courts and punishable by no more than one year in jail.

no-bill
The decision of a grand jury not to indict an accused person due to insufficient evidence. Also called "no true bill."

nolo contendere
Latin for "I do not wish to contend." The defendant neither admits nor denies committing the crime, but agrees to be punished as if guilty. This type of plea cannot be used as an admission of guilt if a civil case is held after the criminal trial.

pillory
A wooden frame with holes for securing the head and hands that was used to secure and expose an offender to public derision.

prejudicial error
An error affecting the outcome of a trial.

presentence report
An account prepared by a probation officer that assists the sentencing court in deciding an appropriate sentence for a convicted defendant. The report includes the defendant's prior, if any, criminal history; relevant personal circumstances; the appropriate classification of the defendant and the offense under the established system; the variety of sentences and programs available; and the offense's impact on the victim.

preventive detention
The jailing of a defendant awaiting trial, usually in order to protect an individual or the public.

***prima facie* case**
A case established by evidence sufficient enough to establish the fact in question unless it is rebutted.

Prohibition
The period from Jan. 29, 1920, to Dec. 5, 1933, during which the manufacture, transportation, and sale of alcoholic beverages was made illegal in the United States by the Eighteenth Amendment. Enforcement legislation was entitled the National Prohibition Act or Volstead Act.

sheriff
From the English words shire and reeve (king's agent). An official of a county or parish who primarily carries out judicial duties.

socialization
A process by which individuals acquire a personal identity and learn the norms, values, behavior, and social skills appropriate to their society.

sociological imagination
Refers to the idea that we must look beyond the obvious to evaluate how our social location influences how we see society. One's race, age, gender, and social-economic status are thought to influence values and perspectives.

true bill
The decision of a grand jury that sufficient evidence exists to indict an accused person.

U.S. Border Patrol
The mobile uniformed law enforcement arm of the Immigration and Naturalization Service. Its primary mission is to detect and prevent the illegal entry of foreign-born persons into the United States.

U.S. Customs Service
The primary enforcement agency protecting U.S. borders and dealing with smuggling, imports, and exports.

U.S. Marshals Service (Federal Marshals)
Created in 1789, the agency protects federal courts and ensures the effective operation of the judicial system. The agency also carries out fugitive investigations, custody and transportation of federal prisoners, security for government witnesses, and asset seizure in federal forfeitures.

U.S. Secret Service
A federal investigative law enforcement agency authorized to protect the president and other U.S. government officials and visiting officials. The agency also investigates financial fraud and counterfeiting.

war on drugs
A policy aimed at reducing the sale and use of illegal drugs. The war metaphor is used to illustrate how serious the drug problem has become in the United States. The war on drugs is fought on many levels, but the criminal justice system spends enormous resources on this problem.

warrant
A writ issued by a judicial official that authorizes an officer to perform a specified act required for the administration of justice, such as an arrest or search.

Short Answer Questions

What are some of the reasons that we might have an inaccurate concept of the nature and frequency of crime? How might C. Wright Mills' sociological imagination help in developing a more accurate picture of crime?

_____
_____
_____
_____
_____
_____
_____
_____
_____
_____

Why does the criminal justice system have three levels of agencies: federal, state, and local? Would it be more efficient to have one big federal agency? What would be the issues if such a policy were adopted?

_____
_____
_____
_____
_____
_____
_____
_____
_____

The numbers of cases in the criminal justice system decrease as they move from offense to disposition. Why? Is this decrease in the number of cases to be expected or does it signify a problem?

___

Is the criminal justice system really a system? If not, what issues and concerns get in the way of it working as a system? Are these issues and concerns problematic or are they desirable checks and balances designed to ensure that justice is done?

___

In addition to the criminal justice system, what other societal institutions are responsible for social control? Which of these institutions has the greatest potential for producing law-abiding citizens? Is it reasonable to expect the criminal justice system to succeed where these other institutions have failed?

_____

_____

_____

_____

_____

_____

_____

_____

_____

_____

Study Guide Questions

Multiple Choice

1. What is the purposeful commission or omission of criminal acts by employees of a business?
a. white-collar crime
b. corporate crime
c. organized crime
d. street crime

2. What organization administers the local jail?
a. The state bureau of investigation
b. The city police
c. The sheriff's department
d. The Federal Marshals

3. The legal term for "no contest" is
a. *lex talionis.*
b. *voir dire.*
c. *nolo contendere.*
d. *mea culpa.*

4. A no-bill is when a grand jury
a. decides to indict.
b. arrives at a verdict.
c. is hung.
d. decides not to indict.

5. A judge may use a pre-sentence report to
a. decide an offender's sentence.
b. throw out a jury's verdict.
c. embark on a bench trial.
d. re-try the offender.

6. Instead of prison, an offender may be sentenced to this.
a. probation
b. parole
c. capital punishment
d. exile

7. Which of these is a goal of the criminal justice system?
a. persecution
b. socialization
c. probation
d. rehabilitation

8. Which practice results in most cases exiting the criminal justice system?
a. plea bargaining
b. execution
c. trials
d. sentencing hearings

9. Crime that is heavily reported by the media may be known as
a. street crime.
b. sensational crime.
c. inchoate crime.
d. crimes known by the police.

10. Criminal justice officials use this to decide which cases to push further into the criminal justice system.
a. hearings
b. trials
c. discretion
d. grand juries

True/False

1. Corporate crime and white-collar crime are different. _____

2. Because of the excess space in state prisons, state prisoners never serve their sentences in local jails. _____

3. State inmates are never housed in federal prisons. _____

4. The Secret Service has many duties besides protecting the president. _____

5. Defendants are formally charged with a crime at their initial appearance in court. _____

6. The criminal justice system has a single goal with different aspects of the system emphasizing this goal. _____

7. The criminal justice system is one of many societal institutions that maintain civil behavior. _____

8. The criminal justice system must balance the preservation of social order with the preservation of individual rights. _____

9. All crimes are eventually detected. _____

10. The media is not responsible for much of what we think we know about crime. _____

Fill in the Blank

1. Most of law enforcement's authority exists at the _____ level.

2. _____ proceedings are secret, and witnesses can be called to testify against a suspect without the presence of the suspect or the suspect's witnesses.

3. The _____ serves warrants and supplies bailiffs to the courts.

4. Deterrence and retribution are two of the _____ of the criminal justice system.

5. _____ may be described as an action taken by a single person or a group that violates a society's rules so that someone is harmed or that society's interests are harmed.

6. Homicide and assault are two crimes measured by the _____.

7. The _____ is not always equal to the public's perception of crime.

8. When crimes are committed, the _____ must respond in the name of society.

9. The family is the primary institution of _____.

10. Those who are awaiting trial may reside in _____.

Find a Flash

Read the two news flashes in Chapter 1 carefully, noting how they illustrate issues covered in the chapter.

- Secret Service Finds Children describes the role of the Secret Service in federal law enforcement and how the agency's mission includes more than protecting the president.
- White-Collar Crime reviews the cases of two of the most infamous white-collar offenders, Ivan F. Boesky and Michael Milken.

Use the library or search the web to find two news items that exemplify, explain, or even appear to contradict topics from Chapter 1. Write short summaries of these news items in the spaces provided. If possible, find one local story and one national story. Give your news flashes short titles that explain what they are about. Suggested news flash topics are listed below.

Sensational crime
Street crime
Corporate crime
Organized crime
Local law enforcement
State law enforcement
The criminal justice process
Religion
Schools
The media

News Flash #1

Title

News Flash #2

Title

What Agency Am I?

Peruse the following descriptions taken from the websites of federal criminal justice-related agencies, programs, and bureaus. Find the organization that matches it in the list and write it in the blank space provided. Hint: Use the web addresses in the list to check the organizations' websites.

A. I am an independent agency that is "the eyes and ears of the nation and, at times, its hidden hand." I collect intelligence, provide analysis, and conduct covert action at the direction of the president to preempt threats or achieve United States policy objectives. I am responsible to the president and accountable to U.S. citizens through the intelligence oversight committees of the U.S. Congress.

Who Am I? _____

B. In 1970, the federal government established me in response to the growing public demand for cleaner water, air, and land. I seek to protect human health and the environment by developing and enforcing regulations that implement environmental laws enacted by Congress. I also administer grants to state environmental programs and perform environmental research.

Who Am I? _____

C. I enforce federal consumer protection laws that prevent fraud, deception, and unfair business practices, as well as antitrust laws. I also conduct economic research and analysis and contribute to the policy deliberations of Congress, the executive branch, other independent agencies, and state and local governments.

Who Am I? _____

D. I am a Commerce Department agency that manages, conserves, and protects living marine resources within the United States' Exclusive Economic Zone (waters three to 200 miles offshore). I ensure compliance with fisheries regulations and work to reduce wasteful fishing practices. I also play a supportive and advisory role in the management of living marine resources in coastal areas under state jurisdiction and implement international conservation and management measures as appropriate.

Who Am I? _____

E. I am a Department of Homeland Security agency that advises on building codes and flood plain management; helps equip local and state emergency agencies; coordinates the federal response to a disaster; makes disaster assistance available to jurisdictions and individuals; trains emergency managers; supports the nation's fire service; and administers the national flood and crime insurance programs.

Who Am I? _____

F. I am a law enforcement agency that seeks to prevent acts of terrorism by targeting the people, money, and materials that support terrorist and criminal activities. The largest investigative arm of the Department of Homeland Security, I am responsible for identifying and shutting down vulnerabilities in the nation's border, economic, transportation, and infrastructure security.

Who Am I? _____

G. Established in September 2003, I am a partnership between the Department of Homeland Security and public and private sectors that protects the nation's Internet infrastructure. I am responsible for analyzing and reducing cyber threats and vulnerabilities; disseminating cyber threat warning information; and coordinating incident response activities.

Who Am I? _____

List

Bureau of Alcohol, Tobacco, Firearms and Explosives	http://www.atf.gov/
Central Intelligence Agency	http://www.cia.gov
Department of Justice	http://www.usdoj.gov
Environmental Protection Agency	http://www.epa.gov
Federal Emergency Management Agency	http://fema.gov/
Federal Trade Commission	http://www.ftc.gov/
National Marine Fisheries Service	http://www.nmfs.noaa.gov/
U.S. Computer Emergency Readiness Team	http://www.us-cert.gov/
U.S. Immigration and Customs Enforcement	http://www.ice.gov

Word Search

Instructions: Fill in the blanks of the definitions below with the correct word, then find the word in the puzzle!

```
U S B T N T P J T B R R D J S F E R E D N E T N O C O L O N
K C N V U Y E Y K P K D B Y M Y N O L E F T H S L Z Q L G K
T O J D W R Q M J S G N I R O T I N O M C I N O R T C E L E
T R E F Q O O U K Y Q E C K T L L I B O N A G S D O A S F O
G S T U B L L N T M H T F K D Z Q K S A W B C F J Q B T G E
Z J Z P C L M M M E H D M Y L F L J S D L E F Y V L O T V R
G E Q T Q I H B Z Z U L S P T E E D A K C O T S Y T N U O C
Y B O L Y P J K V C S R O N A E M E D S I M A D D H N Z N R
R Y N U T D F O P S T N Z P V R P C O I L U X N U H A J G Q
C N W X E C L E A R A N C E R A T E S X F F I R E H S A I O
Q A T K U R N B V Q T B Q X Z D X T C F J E N Z Q S N D R G
W R E N Y M N O T U A R I G C H L R D T X I G L Z Y W I X J
N R I O I T B A I L I F F L F R Z U T J W E J R V N O X E P
W A A I K L P H J T Q X A J L F V E G D A E C Y W D S M B A
V I Y T Y Q S W I B A X V I Z O N B B W R U M I W O C O T M
C G M A O U H J A Q P R X S C B F I R E R P G J K C C F Y L
K N X Z N E L B Q G T R T A Y M W L R X A L W T U X L Q I R
K M B I U O A M O S O C O S I Q M L N Y N A F U H W H V F E
Y E K L W I I J K Y L T S H A X A L K D T L P R P E F H O T
B N Z A K M P T D L I E M M I C U Q O E I Q N V X C O C T Q
J T I I K C E T E Z Y J W Z V B L T V H Q C S U W H N L K Y
Q X P C J F I P Y R K V X R P P I A U D V Q T Y F O I E K J
R P K O D F M Q I A C Z M T K J F T C R L I E M G G J D H W
E J S S I D Y Z D E K S J L N I S G I I F W H G E X O L V P
Q N J B U C B S L E U G I L N E S M W O M G Q F V N F Q X O
F R T Z X P Q O Z B F H F D M S C G Y O N E L P D H T R X Y
O A T C U J O J I V V C M C L Z U Q W U Z K H Y V N D R Z P
N Q G B S Y W V X U B O O J I U V N T Z V C J C N J P H M Y
B K J E X Z T R E T Z F T K W C I O U L M F E E M X X T B Q
U G C J W N R B F R D P R E J U D I C I A L E R R O R L Z L
```

Definitions

1. An _____ is a court appearance in which the defendant is formally charged with a crime and asked to respond by pleading guilty, not guilty, or *nolo contendere*.

2. A _____ is an officer of the court responsible for executing writs and processes, making arrests, and keeping order in the court.

3. A declaration of the charges against an accused person that is presented to a grand jury for determination of whether enough evidence exists for an indictment is also called a _____.

4. _____ are the number of crimes that the police have solved.

5. A _____ is a component of a county corrections system that usually holds offenders who have already been sentenced.

6. The power of a judge, public official, or law enforcement officer to make decisions on issues within legal guidelines is called _____.

7. _____ is an intermediate punishment in which the offender remains in the community but must wear an electronic device that allows the authorities to monitor his or her whereabouts.

8. A _____ is a crime punishable by a term in state or federal prison and sometimes by death.

9. A _____ is a crime this is less serious than a felony, usually tried in the lowest local courts, and punishable by no more than one year in jail.

10. A _____ is the decision of a grand jury not to indict an accused person due to insufficient evidence.

11. The _____, a wooden frame with holes for securing the head and hands, was used to secure and expose an offender to public derision.

12. An error that affects the outcome of a trial is a _____.

13. The word _____ comes from the English words "shire" and "reeve."

14. _____ is the process by which individuals acquire a personal identity and learn the norms, values, behavior, and social skills appropriate to their society.

15. The decision of a grand jury that sufficient evidence exists to indict an accused person is a _____.

16. A _____ is a writ issued by a judicial official that authorizes an officer to perform a specified act required for the administration of justice, such as an arrest or search.

17. _____ was the period from Jan. 29, 1920, to Dec. 5, 1933, during which the manufacture, transportation, and sale of alcoholic beverages was made illegal in the United States by the 18th Amendment.

18. _____ is Latin for "I do not wish to contend."

Chapter 2
The Nature and Measurement of Crime

Learning Objectives
After reading this chapter, you should be able to:

1. Understand how crime is categorized and measured.
2. Discuss crimes against the person.
3. Discuss what should be taken into consideration when measuring property crime.
4. Discuss the relationship of victimless crimes with crimes against the public order.
5. Discuss some of the problems in measuring crime.
6. Discuss the dark figure of crime.
7. Discuss sources of error in the Uniform Crime Reports.
8. Calculate a crime rate.
9. Compare and contrast the UCR, the NIBRS, victimization surveys, and self-report studies.
10. Compare and contrast the effect of crime-measuring efforts on the general public with how the general public affects crime-measuring efforts.

Chapter Summary and Key Concepts
Chapter 2 reviews the way crime is measured and how the level of crime affects the criminal justice system and the public's fear of crime.

Types of Crime
- There are three general types of crime: crimes against the person, crimes against property, and crimes against the public order.
- Crimes against the person carry the most severe penalties and may involve interpersonal disputes, instrumental violence, group violence, chronic violent offenders, political violence, rape and sexual assault, and robbery.
- Crimes against property, which include burglary, larceny/theft, motor vehicle theft, and arson, usually do not carry the same impact as crimes against persons.
- Crimes against the public order offend the sensibilities of some groups of people who have been successful in getting their values encoded into the criminal law.

Measuring Crime
- Crime is measured in four major ways: the Uniform Crime Reports (UCR), the National Incident-Based Reporting System (NIBRS), victimization studies, and self-report studies.
- The Uniform Crime Reports, the largest, most expensive, most comprehensive, and oldest method used to represent the incidence and seriousness of crime, continues to be used to allocate resources, deploy police officers, and report crime levels.
- The two types of error in the UCR are unintentional and intentional.
- The National Incident-Based Reporting System is designed to correct for some of the UCR's flaws, primarily by collecting data on all criminal incidents that take place, not only on the most serious crime.

- Victimization studies ask victims of crime about their experiences, are not as comprehensive as the UCR, and only provide a snapshot of the actual incidences of crime.
- Self-report studies ask offenders to identify the types of crimes they have committed over the past six months or year.
- Homicide, rape, and robbery are separated from other types of crime when the crime rate is discussed.
- Crime rates are calculated so that crime levels may be compared across jurisdictions.
- The eight UCR Part I Offenses are murder and non-negligent manslaughter, forcible rape, robbery, aggravated assault, burglary, larceny/theft, motor vehicle theft, and arson.
- Self-report studies and victimization studies miss or obscure corporate crime, organized crime, drug sales, prostitution, and gambling.
- Larceny/theft, burglary, automobile theft, and arson are measured by criminal justice data-gathering efforts to ascertain their levels of seriousness and frequency.

The Perception of Crime
- The media has facilitated the institutionalization of categories of newly discovered crimes such as stalking.
- A gap exists between the public's fear of crime and the actual threat of crime. Those who have the least to fear are often those who go to the greatest extremes to avoid dangerous situations. Those who are victimized the most are the ones who seem to fear crime the least and engage in high-risk behaviors.

Key Terms

arson
The act of intentionally burning a building. Any death that results from arson is murder, regardless of the arsonist's intention.

burglary
The act of breaking into and entering a building or other structure or vehicle in order to commit a crime. Extreme force is not required, and burglary is not restricted to theft. Any crime committed, such as assault, is considered to be burglary.

crime rate
The number of Crime Index offenses divided by the population of an area, usually given as a rate of crimes per 100,000 people.

dark figure of crime
A metaphor that describes crime that goes unreported to police and criminal justice officials and is never quantified.

larceny
A form of theft in which an offender takes possessions that do not belong to him/her with the intent of keeping them. Some jurisdictions specify "grand larceny" or "petty larceny" based on the value of the stolen items.

National Incident-Based Reporting System (NIBRS)
A crime-reporting system in which each separate offense in a crime is described, including data describing the offender(s), victim(s), and property.

rape
Sexual activity, usually sexual intercourse, that is forced on the person of another party without his/her consent, usually under threat of harm. Sexual activity conducted with a person who is younger than a specified age or incapable of valid consent because of mental illness, mental handicap, intoxication, unconsciousness, or deception is called statutory rape.

robbery
The removal of property from a person by violence or by threat of violence.

serial murder
Homicides of a sequence of victims committed by an offender in three or more separate events occurring over a period of time.

sexual assault
Sexual contact that is committed without the other party's consent or with a party who is not capable of giving consent (such as a child or mentally handicapped individual).

terrorism
The use or threat of violence against a state or other political entity in order to coerce.

Uniform Crime Reports (UCR)
An annual publication by the Federal Bureau of Investigation that uses data from all participating law enforcement agencies in the U.S. to summarize the incidence and rate of reported crime.

victim precipitation
A situation in which a crime victim plays an active role in initiating a crime or escalating it.

victimization studies
Surveys that attempt to measure the extent of crime by interviewing people who have suffered crime.

Short Answer Questions

Which crimes are more harmful to society: crimes against the person, crimes against property, or crimes against public order? Which of these types of crimes is most prevalent? Which would you least like to be a victim of?

_____

_____

_____

_____

_____

_____

_____

_____

_____

For what reasons might individuals not report a crime? Is a behavior really a crime if no one reports it?

_____

_____

_____

_____

_____

_____

_____

_____

What are the differences between the Uniform Crime Reports Part I and Part II Offenses? Why is the measurement of crime categorized in this manner?

What are the advantages and disadvantages of using Uniform Crime Reports, self-reported crime studies, and victimization studies to measure the crime problem? Are any of these measures of crime better or more accurate than the others?

Is a fear of crime something that should be possessed by reasonable people? Who has the most to fear from crime? The least? How does the media influence our fear of crime?

___
___
___
___
___
___
___
___
___

Study Guide Questions

Multiple Choice

1. Which of the following is not typified as a "crime against the person?"
   a. homicide
   b. arson
   c. robbery
   d. assault

2. What is the unlawful entry of a structure to commit a felony or theft?
   a. larceny/theft
   b. robbery
   c. breaking-and-entering
   d. burglary

3. Which behavior does not fit into the category of crimes against the public order?
   a. terrorism
   b. vagrancy
   c. disorderly conduct
   d. liquor-law violations

4. Which crime is one of the UCR's eight Part I Offenses?
   a. embezzlement
   b. simple assault

c. vandalism
d. non-negligent manslaughter

5. One of the problems of attempting to measure crime is that
a. not all crimes are reported.
b. too many crimes are reported.
c. some of the reports are not really crimes.
d. there are many measurement techniques.

6. Crimes that occur but that do not get reported are known as the
a. unknown crimes.
b. dark measure of crime.
c. dense figure of crime.
d. dark figure of crime.

7. This is the most extensive and useful measure of crime available.
a. victimization surveys
b. Uniform Crime Reports
c. self-report studies
d. arrest reports

8. This is necessary in order to compare crime across jurisdictions.
a. studying crime reports
b. calculating the crime rate
c. accessing crime statistics
d. talking to victims

9. This instrument gathers data on each criminal act committed within the same complex of behavior.
a. the Uniform Crime Reports
b. victimization surveys
c. National Incident-Based Reporting System
d. arrest reports

10. This is a method for trying to understand the level of unreported crime.
a. media reports
b. victimization surveys
c. crime-rate calculations
d. arrest reports

True/False

1. Legal categorizations of crimes are the best indicators of the nature of the crime problem. _____

2. The National Incident-Based Reporting System gathers data on all offenses committed in a multi-crime incident. _____

3. Considering victimization is not a way to understand crime. _____

4. All crimes involve a discernable victim. _____

5. Victimization surveys do not provide a comprehensive account of crime. _____

6. Burglary is different from larceny/theft. _____

7. Measuring crime is easy. _____

8. The Uniform Crime Reports provide a useful picture of crime in the United States. _____

9. Assault is considered a crime against public order. _____

10. Serial murder is uncommon. _____

Fill in the Blank

1. The _____ feature intentional and unintentional sources of error.

2. One must calculate the crime rate in order to compare crime across _____.

3. The _____ requires a much greater level of detail in the reporting of crime than does the Uniform Crime Reports.

4. Auto theft is a crime against _____.

5. Society has rules, regulations, norms, folkways, and _____ that dictate what is acceptable behavior and what is not.

6. Capital punishment is reserved for those who commit crimes against the _____.

7. Offenders sometimes use _____ violence as means to another unlawful end.

8. The _____ is better than the _____ in helping officials estimate the dark figure of crime.

9. The National Crime Victimization Survey gathers data on subgroups of _____.

10: _____ is when a victim is active in initiating or escalating a crime.

Find a Flash
Read the two news flashes in Chapter 2 carefully, noting how they illustrate issues covered in the chapter.

- *Lies, Damn Lies, and Statistics* describes crime how statistics can be skewed, changing the picture of crime in a jurisdiction.
- *Fear* reviews the relationship between crime and the fear of crime.

Use the library or search the web to find two news items that exemplify, explain, or even appear to contradict topics from Chapter 2. Write short summaries of these news items in the spaces provided. If possible, find one local story and one national story. Give your news flashes short titles that explain what they are about. Suggested news flash topics are listed below.

Crimes against the person
Crimes against property
Crimes against public order
Uniform Crime Reports
National Incident-Based Reporting System
Victimization surveys
Self-report studies

News Flash #1

Title

News Flash #2

Title

What Agency Am I?

Peruse the following descriptions taken from the websites of federal criminal justice-related agencies, programs, and bureaus. Find the organization that matches it in the list and write it in the blank space provided. Hint: Use the web addresses in the list to check the organizations' websites.

A. Part of the Justice Department's Office of Justice Programs, I support local criminal justice strategies to achieve safe communities. My goals include providing training and technical assistance supporting efforts to prevent crime, drug abuse, and violence at the national, state, and local levels; reducing the availability of illegal weapons; and assisting states in the design and implementation of effective correctional options for nonviolent offenders.

Who Am I? _____

B. I am a component of the Justice Department's Office of Justice Programs that collects, analyzes, and publishes information on crime, criminal offenders, victims of crime, and the operation of justice systems at all government levels.

Who Am I? _____

C. As the investigative arm of the Department of Justice, I protect and defend the United States against terrorist and foreign intelligence threats; uphold and enforce criminal laws; and provide leadership and criminal justice services to federal, state, municipal, and international agencies and partners.

Who Am I?_____

List
Bureau of Justice Assistance   http://www.ojp.usdoj.gov/bja
Bureau of Justice Statistics   http://www.ojp.usdoj.gov/bjs
Federal Bureau of Investigation   http://www.fbi.gov
Federal Trade Commission   http://www.ftc.gov
U.S. Computer Emergency Readiness Team   http://www.us-cert.gov
U.S. Immigration and Customs Enforcement   http://www.ice.gov
United States Marshals Service   http://www.usdoj.gov/marshals

Word Search

Instructions: Fill in the blanks of the definitions below with the correct word, then find the word in the puzzle!

```
R B O W C F G N G T L H Q Z U Z Z G W G Q Z Y J P N H D C A
Y G H Z A P H C U O L D F B E S G W Z K Q T Q Q V A F C D F
Y H U V B H S C E V A H A C W X B D C O I C T O J B Z S J E
V Z B H K S B P N Z R D I K J D S U G H J U V R N Z U A R U
W W F W X U H L Y T C D W R F J R E E X A N E O M E K Z P M
G A U F I V Z Y G X E F E H J Z H V G N G D I X J O K G N J
Z B M S V B T B Y N N K Q D F Z Z V L U R T K E H T B E X D
Q D J H S O Y X R I Y V E Q W Y A Y T U A L M R E F D K L O
K E C G N F I W Y B Q P V X R F E O M T U Z U R A S B N M Q
Y E C X Y U F Q Y W M I J P F N U L I Y L R R Y H P W P B O
U R I E H O O Y N J I J U L W A A P E J R O Q A C F E R B Q
Y A O X Z I U W V X C B U G H I I C G B R A P B A T P B Q A
M G R B J E B U Q T Y K P C R C Y J P I A A L C Q C U A L J
L P F P B K L I R B I G T E E H P M S S F W J G M F E E E H
M O Z F S E C D P W R W S R K X D M P V H X X P R O R Y A J
E X O W V O R W J I L T P U S Y O S Y K I Q F X X U R Q W B
B J Y R Z N T Y Q J Q M B J S Z G X F I O K U V Z T B O B D
Q Z G R J E G O Q W I C J D A R K F I G U R E O F C R I M E
S S R O R X Q S F T T L U A S S A L A U X E S D O X X C K S
F F K N O S M Z C Y N V Q D T Y Q N L S V R K D U N P K J A
P W O I V X Y I E Z H G A V Z I J W J P K F O I D V C T L G
H E D T O L V U U N I F O R M C R I M E R E P O R T S S Y Y
L X U O G N Q Z G M D Q E T A R E M I R C B F C R Y U X X V
O N W L M X F N G V O Z Q D J W D P D V Z V N G W W Y M U R
X Z A I Z L A V B F T K V K K V O Z M F D O Z Z Q H J N Y X
A L Y C J Z L L B U F B B Y R K V N L Z S A X J S M B V R N
V I C T I M I Z A T I O N S T U D I E S P J R Q O Q W G V F
V Z B T E A I H H H O N F M O M Z U B X S B A B F S H Y U S
Y N O S R A Z T S H P D D E O S K K K E M Z P O F N F K H C
V T G R Z C C D G R A F M B V O V Z K D K X T K P D A J K Q
```

Definitions

1. _____ is the act of intentionally burning a building.

2. Breaking into and entering a building or other structure or vehicle in order to commit a crime is _____.

3. _____ is the number of Crime Index offenses divided by the population of an area, usually given as a rate of crimes per 100,000 people.

4. The _____ is a metaphor that describes crime that goes unreported to police and criminal justice officials and is never quantified.

5. A form of theft in which an offender takes possessions that do not belong to him/her with the intent of keeping them is _____.

6. _____ is sexual activity, usually sexual intercourse, that is forced on the person of another party without his/her consent, usually under threat of harm.

7. The removal of property from a person by violence or by threat of violence is _____.

8. The homicides of a sequence of victims committed by an offender in three or more separate events occurring over a period of time is called _____.

9. _____ is sexual contact that is committed without the other party's consent or with a party who is not capable of giving consent.

10. The use or threat of violence against a state or other political entity in order to coerce is _____.

11. The acronym for _____ is "UCR."

12. _____ are surveys that attempt to measure the extent of crime by interviewing people who have suffered crime.

13. A situation in which a crime victim plays an active role in initiating a crime or escalating it is called _____.

Chapter 3
Theories of Crime

Learning Objectives
After reading this chapter, you should be able to:

1. Discuss the role of demonology in early explanations of crime.
2. Discuss the strengths and weaknesses of the classical school of criminology.
3. Describe Cesare Beccaria's nine principles that should guide our thinking about crime and society.
4. Discuss the role of Charles Darwin in the positivist school of criminology.
5. Discuss early biological theories of crime versus modern biological theories of crime.
6. Describe Sigmund Freud's impact on criminological thought.
7. Discuss the Chicago school of thought.
8. Describe Merton's adaptations to blocked means of achieving cultural goals.
9. Explain Sykes' and Matza's five techniques of neutralization.
10. Discuss the importance of Karl Marx's ideas in criminological theory.

Chapter Summary and Key Concepts
Chapter 3 reviews traditional and new theories of crime that attempt to describe the variety of deviant and criminal behavior.

Ideas About Theories of Crime
- Crime is socially defined. What is considered a crime at one place and time may be considered normal or even heroic behavior in another context.
- The earliest explanations for deviant behavior attributed crime to supernatural forces. A common method to determine guilt or innocence was trial by ordeal.
- Although theories of crime causation and the workings of the legal and criminal justice systems are of limited utility, there are theories that can explain some crime.
- Many theories of crime have failed to provide reasonable explanations.

The Classical School of Criminology
- The classical school of criminology, which argues that people freely choose to engage in crime, is embodied primarily in the works of Cesare Beccaria and Jeremy Bentham.
- Beccaria presented nine principles that should guide our thinking about crime and the way society responds to lawbreakers.
- According to Bentham's utilitarianism theory, people are guided by a desire for pleasure and aversion to pain.

The Positivist School of Criminology
- The positivist school of criminology uses scientific techniques to study crime and criminals and focuses on what factors compel offenders to commit crimes.
- The positivist school comprises many types of theories of crime, including biological, psychological, sociological, and critical sociological.

Biological Theories of Crime
- Many biological theories of crime have been discredited. These include phrenology, Lombroso's atavisms, Hooton's work with physiology, Sheldon's somatotyping, and XYY syndrome (as a causal factor of criminal behavior).
- Phrenology was a technique in which a subject's personality was assessed by the size and pattern of the bumps on his or her skull.
- Cesare Lombroso used the term *atavisms* to describe the physical differences he believed he found between offenders and non-offenders.
- Earnest Hooton also studied the relationship between physiology and crime. He claimed that the physical features of offenders were different from those of non-offenders.
- William Sheldon used the term *somatotyping* to describe three variations of the body, endomorph, mesomorph, and ectomorph, and claimed that body-type was an indication of behavior.
- XYY syndrome refers to males who are born with an extra Y chromosome. It has been postulated that XYY males are more prone to commit crime.
- Currently, researchers are examining three areas in order to determine if some people commit crimes for physical reasons: hormones, brain structure, and brain chemistry.

Psychological Theories
- Sigmund Freud developed a psychological paradigm that focused on unconscious forces and drives. He contended that the personality comprises three parts: the id, ego, and superego.
- B.F. Skinner's theory of behaviorism, based on the psychological principle of operant conditioning, states that behavior is determined by rewards and punishments.

Sociological Theories of Crime
- Sociological theories focus on the social situation or environment as a cause of crime.
- Chicago school researchers concluded that social disorganization causes crime.
- Edwin Sutherland developed differential association theory, which claims that crime is learned.
- Ronald Akers contends that crime is learned according to the principles of operant conditioning.
- Robert Merton's strain theory of delinquency was influenced by French sociologist Emile Durkheim's theory of anomie or "normlessness."
- Travis Hirschi's social control theory explores why most people do not commit crimes.
- Gresham Sykes and David Matza developed neutralization theory to describe how offenders deflect feelings of blame and shame.
- Edwin Lemert helped develop labeling theory, which contends that people commit deviant behavior because they consider themselves "outsiders" and attempt to live up to that label.

Critical Sociological Theories of Crime
- The term "critical theory" describes a range of perspectives that consider social justice as a legitimate end.

- Criminologists who study Karl Marx's ideas of social control point out that those in power control the making and the enforcement of the law.
- Feminism examines how women are treated differently from men in a society dominated by male power structures.
- Much of what is reported about female offenders and female criminal justice system practitioners is based on the study of males.
- Critical race theory observes that people of color are over-represented in the criminal justice system and suggests that race is a crucial variable for scholars to examine when attempting to explain the dynamics of the criminal justice system.

Key Terms

anomie
A condition in which a people or society undergoes a breakdown of social norms and values.

atavism
The appearance in a person of features thought to be from earlier stages of human evolution. Popularized by Cesare Lombroso.

behaviorism
The assessment of human psychology via the examination of objectively observable and quantifiable actions, as opposed to subjective mental states.

Chicago school
Criminological theories that rely, in part, on individuals' demographics and geographic location to explain criminal behavior.

classical school of criminology
A set of criminological theories that uses the idea of free will to explain criminal behavior.

differential association theory
States that crime is learned. Children learn crime from other children. Developed by Edwin Sutherland.

false consciousness
An attitude held by members of a class that does not accurately reflect the reality of that class's existence. A term associated with Karl Marx.

labeling theory
A perspective that considers recidivism to be a consequence, in part, of the negative labels applied to offenders.

neutralization theory
A perspective that states that juvenile delinquents have feelings of guilt when involved in illegal activities. Illegal behavior is episodic and delinquents drift between legal and illegal activities. The delinquent sets aside his/her own legal and moral values in order to drift into illegal activities.

operant conditioning
The alteration of behavior by giving a subject rewards or punishments for a specified action until the subject associates the action with pleasure or pain.

positivist school of criminology
A set of criminological theories that uses scientific techniques to study crime and criminals.

rational choice theory
A theory that states that people choose criminal behavior consciously. The theory also states that people may choose to commit crime upon realizing that the crime's benefits probably outweigh the consequences of breaking the law.

social control theory
A perspective that seeks not to explain why people break the law, but instead explores what keeps most people from breaking the law. Associated with Travis Hirschi.

somatotyping
The use of body types and physical characteristics to classify human personalities.

strain theory
A hypothesis in which the causes of crime can be connected to the pressure on culturally or materially disadvantaged groups or individuals to achieve the goals held by society, even if the means to those goals require the breaking of laws. Based on Emile Durkheim's theory of anomie.

trial by ordeal
An ancient custom found in many cultures in which the accused was required to perform a test to prove guilt or innocence. The outcome of the test was considered to be decided by a divine authority.

utilitarianism
A theory associated with Jeremy Bentham that states that people will choose not to commit crime when the pain of punishment outweighs the benefit derived from the crime.

XYY syndrome
A condition in which a male is born with an extra Y chromosome. Such males tend to be tall, have difficulties with language, and have relatively low IQs. The condition was once thought to cause criminal behavior.

Short Answer Questions

Cesare Lombroso developed a theory of crime based on the physical characteristics of the offender. How has this search for the physical difference between offenders and non-offenders progressed since Lombroso's time? Has modern science gotten any closer to finding a physical marker in offenders?

Cesare Beccaria and Jeremy Bentham are credited with developing the classical school of criminology. What does the perspective treat as the proper focus of criminology, the crime or the offender? How does the classical school of criminology still affect the criminal justice system?

The Chicago school of sociology contributed the basis for several theories of criminology. Explain how its emphasis on the social disorganization of urban life influenced the study of criminal behavior.

Compare and contrast Merton's strain theory of crime with Hirschi's social control theory. What factors do each of these theories deem to be problematic?

To what extent does the modern feminist movement help society address crime? Has it increased opportunities for females as either offenders or as practitioners in the criminal justice system?

Study Guide Questions

Multiple Choice
1. Which criminal investigation technique has been discredited?
a. atavisms
b. eyewitness testimony
c. fiber evidence
d. interrogation

2. What is an example of a somatotype?
a. supermorph
b. ectogram
c. ectomorph
d. altomorph

3. The classical school of criminology is based, in part, on the work of this scholar.
a. Franz Joseph Gall
b. Donald Sutherland
c. Karl Marx
d. Cesare Beccaria

4. According to this theory by Jeremy Bentham, people are guided by their desire for pleasure and aversion to pain.
a. phrenology
b. utilitarianism theory
c. labeling theory
d. pain theory

5. This criminological discipline is an outgrowth of the rise of the scientific method.
a. the positivist school
b. the classical school
c. Marxism
d. the Chicago school

6. This Italian physician believed that criminals were physically different from the rest of the population.
a. Cesare Lombroso
b. Cesare Beccaria
c. Ceasar Romero
d. Jeremy Bentham

7. The theory that behavior is determined by rewards and punishments is called
a. XYY theory.
b. Marxism.
c. labeling theory.
d. behaviorism.

8. The criminologists from this school did not believe that crime is individual in nature.
a. the positivist school
b. the feminist school
c. Chicago school
d. the classical school

9. This theory developed by Edwin Sutherland is one of the most popular theories of delinquency.
a. differential association theory
b. strain theory
c. anomie
d. social control theory

10. This theory does not ask why offenders commit crimes, but why most people do not.
a. neutralization theory
b. social control theory
c. labeling theory
d. false consciousness

True/False

1. According to Bentham, society drives offenders to commit crime. _____

2. Cesare Lombroso believed that body type determined behavior. _____

3. XYY syndrome has not been proven to have any effect on criminal behavior. _____

4. Modeling involves an offender's behavior being shaped and molded by the criminal justice system. _____

5. According to Sykes and Matza, two neutralization techniques are denial of injury and denial of victim. _____

6. False consciousness, according to Karl Marx, is an attitude held by people that does not accurately reflect the reality of their existence. _____

7. A strength of criminological theory is its reliance on the study of male subjects. _____

8. Critical race theory is based on the observation that people of color are over-represented at every decision point of the criminal justice system. _____

9. Ernest Hooton's physiology-based theory is widely used in the criminal justice system. _____

10. The criminal justice system eschews supernatural explanations of crime. _____

Fill in the Blank

1. _____ believed that punishments should be proportional to crimes.

2. Skinner's _____ theory is based on the psychological principle of operant conditioning.

3. According to differential association theory, crime is _____.

4. Robert Merton's strain theory was influenced by Emile Durkheim's theory of _____.

5. _____ theory seeks to explain how delinquents drift between conventional lifestyles and delinquent ones.

6. According to Bentham's _____ theory, people are guided by desire for pleasure and aversion to pain.

7. In labeling theory, there is an important distinction between _____ and _____ deviation.

8. According to _____, women's opportunities to commit crime are influenced by the greater controls they experience in society.

9. _____ used the term *somatotyping* to describe the classification of three body variations.

10. _____ believed that healthy people have a proper balance of id, ego, and superego.

Find a Flash
Read the two news flashes in Chapter 3 carefully, noting how they illustrate issues covered in the chapter.

- *Lies, Lies, Lies* covers law enforcement's search for a method to discern when a suspect is lying, including polygraph tests and a relatively recent technique called "brain fingerprinting."
- *Crime and the Economy* examines the economy's apparent connection to crime rates.

Use the library or search the web to find two news items that exemplify, explain, or even appear to contradict topics from Chapter 3. Write short summaries of these news items in the spaces provided. If possible, find one local story and one national story. Give your news flashes short titles that explain what they are about. Suggested news flash topics are listed below.

The classical school of criminology
The positivist school of criminology
Biological theories of crime
Psychological theories of crime
Sociological theories of crime
Critical sociological theories of crime

News Flash #1

Title

News Flash #2

Title

What Agency Am I?

Peruse the following descriptions taken from the websites of federal criminal justice-related agencies, programs, and bureaus. Find the organization that matches it in the list and write it in the blank space provided. Hint: Use the web addresses in the list to check the organizations' websites.

A. I am a research, development, and evaluation agency of the Justice Department that researches crime control and justice issues, particularly at the state and local levels. I also evaluate programs, policies, and technologies.

Who Am I? _____

B. I am a federal resource that offers justice and substance abuse information to support research, policy, and program development worldwide.

Who Am I? _____

C. I was created in 1929 by the International Association of Chiefs of Police to provide reliable, uniform crime statistics for the nation. Today, several statistical publications, such as *Crime in the United States*, are produced from my data, which is provided by nearly 17,000 law enforcement agencies across the United States.

Who Am I?_____

List

Bureau of Justice Assistance	http://www.ojp.usdoj.gov/bja
Federal Bureau of Investigation	http://www.fbi.gov
Federal Trade Commission	http://www.ftc.gov
National Criminal Justice Reference Service	http://www.ncjrs.org
National Institute of Justice	http://www.ojp.usdoj.gov/nij
Uniform Crime Reports (FBI)	http://www.fbi.gov/ucr/ucr.htm
United States Marshals Service	http://www.usdoj.gov/marshals

Word Search

Instructions: Fill in the blanks of the definitions below with the correct word, then find the word in the puzzle!

```
N P S J H L R I N H X O L F A T G C G I P X N C H S Y B J W
C Z Y S W V F Q Y J C H Y B G N I P Y T O T A M O S R H C Q
M L R R Y B H F U U I U A P H M J M U C K W J Q F P Y K R T
A E Q A E V G G I U I Y N C E O Z S H X G M H H V I W L V R
Y I P D S T Z R G Z X J O O R H I W U R S Y B A N J L O O I
R D I G J F H W B F Y J M Z F R P P X I O R E F C U L O F A
O Q F Q R A I S N P Y U I M O Y U N R G O O U V H M L H F L
E E M K F L E X K T S T E A I I Z O W N R E E Q S T L C Z B
H J L W G S H F L A Y I N V N T I K F I C H Z D G Z K S C Y
T R T U L E X L D C N X G B G V R L B N H T Q R A L Y O G O
L C T A X C D P E V D M Q I A N H A T O R N A G G N Y G S R
O W R J C O R O Y W R E A H E Z G M X I C O I I I E S A F D
R G A P N N M S Y H O D E W M O Z B Q T L I P L V B A C H E
T L H O S S E G E R M B T X L A V P U I A T L P M D L I O A
N C M S V C D T J D E L Y I R K B Q L D S A N I G I N H V L
O Z X I L I O G R L A J C C L Y E B W N S Z H P V D A C G A
C S M T V O R M W S W V L T P E U Q S O I I G N J T G M S Y
L Y S I F U B I G C T B A I Z Y F N K C C L H Q Q X U B T A
A T I V N S W B Y J U E B J L J Q X L T A A X R Q I W M P T
I Z N I U N O Q H Y N D E H Z S D P T N L R I T W D P Z J N
C J A S T E H N Z D O A L R S H A X N A S T O R K A S E E L
O F I T A S L O W Z T E I R W Y N K D R C U E C R L S Q S T
S N R S W S G S M A V J N F G G O E K E H E E X Q L A S Y W
C U A C D B Y Z V M Q X G L I V Y L P P O N J D I C M F B P
V I T H B H Q I C L O S T F O S R I N O O S G Z V X Y U Q R
S S I O Q Q S F Y R O E H T E C I O H C L A N O I T A R C I
N Z L O B M Q L A C N Y E A K F T N G X Q M T O L S S V G S
S E I L S X S I S I R O O N K R C X Y R O E H T N I A R T S
Z W T A J U B C J U P A R W L Q R O N D D E V B P C K U U G
O J U S R H T T Y N E F Y G O L O U P F N V S W D S O P M V
```

Definitions

1. _____ is a condition in which a people or society undergoes a breakdown of social norms and values.

2. Cesare Lombroso popularized the theory of _____.

3. The assessment of human psychology via the examination of objectively observable and quantifiable actions, as opposed to subjective mental states, is _____.

4. The _____ is a set of criminological theories that rely, in part, on individuals' demographics and geographic location to explain criminal behavior.

5. The _____ of criminology is a set of criminological theories that uses the idea of free will to explain criminal behavior.

45

6. _____ is an attitude held by members of a class that does not accurately reflect the reality of that class's existence.

7. _____ is a perspective that considers recidivism to be a consequence, in part, of the negative labels applied to offenders.

8. _____ is a perspective that states that juvenile delinquents have feelings of guilt when involved in illegal activities.

9. _____ is the alteration of behavior by giving a subject rewards or punishments for a specified action until the subject associates the action with pleasure or pain.

10. The _____ of criminology is a set of criminological theories that uses scientific techniques to study crime and criminals.

11. _____ is a perspective that states that people choose criminal behavior consciously.

12. _____ is a perspective that seeks not to explain why people break the law, but instead explores what keeps most people from breaking the law.

13. The use of body types and physical characteristics to classify human personalities is _____.

14. _____ is based on Emile Durkheim's theory of anomie.

15. _____ is an ancient custom found in many cultures in which the accused was required to perform a test to prove guilt or innocence.

16. _____ states that people will choose not to commit crime when the pain of punishment outweighs the benefit derived from the crime.

17. _____ is a condition in which a male is born with an extra Y chromosome.

Chapter 4
Criminal Law

Learning Objectives
After reading this chapter, you should be able to:
1. Discuss where the criminal law fits into the continuum of social control.
2. Discuss the development and foundations of criminal law.
3. Discuss the role of common law in the modern criminal justice system.
4. Discuss the relationship of common law and precedent.
5. Discuss the role of the Constitution in the law and its relationship to state constitutions.
6. Discuss the role of the Bill of Rights.
7. Contrast statutes with administrative rules.
8. Discuss the differences between criminal law and civil law.
9. Discuss inchoate offenses.
10. Discuss concurrence and strict liability.

Chapter Summary and Key Concepts
Chapter 4 examines the criminal law and reviews the establishment of criminal responsibility and criminal defense.

The Development of Law
- The criminal law as a form of social control occupies one end of a continuum: folkways ⟶ mores ⟶ norms ⟶ laws.
- The criminal justice system is governed by the criminal law, which developed in a sporadic and uneven fashion.
- The criminal law can trace its influences to the Code of Hammurabi (c. 1780 B.C.E.), the first known set of written laws.
- The four sources of law are common law, constitutions, statutes, and administrative rules.

Common Law
- The early North American colonies adopted the principles of English common law, which called for cases to be decided on precedent. Precedent helped to develop consistency in the law.
- Four issues guide precedent: predictability, reliability, efficiency, and equality.
- Instead of being expressly specified by a constitution or a legislature, the common law is based on judicial decisions.
- Common Law is sometimes called case law, judiciary law, judge-made law, customary law, or unwritten law.

Criminal Law
- The criminal law represents the state against individuals.
- The first 10 amendments, the Bill of Rights, are an especially important cornerstone of the criminal law.
- Substantive laws proscribing murder, rape, robbery, and the like originate from statutes provided by Congress and state legislatures.

- Three criteria determine what behaviors are made criminal: legal enforceability, legal effects, and the existence of other means to protect society from undesirable behavior.

Administrative Rules, Procedural Law, and Civil Law
- A number of agencies that govern health, customs, the environment, and parole promulgate administrative rules that are enforceable by the criminal law.
- Procedural law controls how criminal justice system officials enforce substantive law.
- Civil law is concerned with disputes between individuals. It deals with contracts, personal property, maritime law, and commercial law.

Classifications of Crime
- Crime can be classified into three categories: felonies, misdemeanors, and inchoate offenses.
- Felonies, the most serious types of crime, include murder, rape, assault, larceny, arson, and other offenses at the state and federal level.
- Misdemeanors are less serious than felonies and are subject to less severe penalties. Usually, the maximum incarceration for a misdemeanor is up to one year in jail.
- A crime could be categorized as either a misdemeanor or felony, depending on the circumstances.
- Inchoate offenses are crimes that do not have to be completed in order for the offender to be arrested, charged, and punished. Two examples are conspiracy and attempt.

Criminal Defense
- Three elements, called the *corpus delicti* (meaning "body of the crime"), must be present in order for an act to be labeled a crime: the criminal act (*actus reus*); criminal intent (*mens rea*); and the relationship between *actus reus* and *mens rea* (concurrence).
- Strict liability offenses are the primary exception to the requirement of the presence of both *mens rea* and *actus reus*. Strict liability offenses usually are crimes that concern the public's welfare.
- Six arguments can be used in the defense against a criminal indictment: my client did not do it; my client did it, but is not responsible because he or she is insane; my client did it but has a good excuse; my client did it but has a good reason; my client did it but should be acquitted because the police or the prosecutor cheated; my client did it but was influenced by outside forces.

Key Terms

actus reus
"Guilty deed." The physical action of a crime.

alibi
A defense that involves the defendant(s) claiming not to have been at the scene of a crime when that crime was committed.

Bill of Rights
The first 10 amendments to the U.S. Constitution, which guarantee fundamental rights and privileges to citizens.

civil law
The law that governs private rights as opposed to the law that governs criminal issues.

Code of Hammurabi
An ancient code instituted by Hammurabi, a ruler of Babylonia, dealing with criminal and civil matters.

common law
Sometimes called case law, judiciary law, judge-made law, customary law, or unwritten law, common law is based on customs and general principles and is included in case law. Common law may also be used as precedent or for matters not addressed by statute.

concurrence
The coexistence of *actus reus* and *mens rea*.

corpus delicti
"Body of the crime." The crime itself.

double jeopardy
The prosecution in the same jurisdiction of a defendant for an offense for which the defendant has already been prosecuted and convicted or acquitted. Also refers to multiple punishments for a single offense. The Fifth Amendment states that no person will "be subject for the same offense to be twice put in jeopardy of life or limb."

habeas corpus
A writ issued to bring a party before the court.

inchoate offense
An offense comprising acts necessary to commit another crime.

infancy
In legal terminology, refers to a child who has not yet reached a specific age. Almost all states end infancy at the age of 18.

insanity defense
A defense that attempts to give physical or psychological reasons that a defendant cannot comprehend his/her criminal actions, their harm(s), or their punishment.

Magna Carta
"Great charter." A guarantee of liberties signed by King John of England in 1215 that influenced many modern legal and constitutional principles.

mens rea
"Guilty mind." Intent or knowledge to commit a crime.

penal code
A code of laws that deals with crimes and the punishments for them.

precedent
A prior legal decision used as a basis for deciding a later, similar case.

procedural law
Laws that prescribe the methods for their enforcement and use.

stare decisis
The doctrine under which courts adhere to legal precedent.

statute
A law enacted by a legislature.

statutory law
The type of law that is enacted by legislatures, as opposed to common law.

statutory rape
Sexual activity conducted with a person who is younger than a specified age or incapable of valid consent because of mental illness, mental handicap, intoxication, unconsciousness, or deception.

strict liability
Responsibility for a crime without intention to commit a crime. *Mens rea* is not required in strict liability findings.

substantive law
The law that defines rights and proscribes certain actions (crimes).

tort law
A large area of the law that deals with civil acts, other than breach of contract, that cause harm and injury. Tort law includes libel, slander, assault, trespass, and negligence.

Short Answer Questions

Trace the development of criminal law. What were the contributions of the Code of Hammurabi and the Magna Carta?

What are the various sources of the law? Which of these sources is the most important?

What is the difference between substantive law and procedural law? Which applies to offenders and which applies to criminal justice practitioners?

What three elements must be present in order for an act to be labeled a crime? Provide an example of a crime that includes all three of these features.

List and discuss six arguments a defense attorney might use to mitigate the culpability of the defendant. Which of these arguments is the most convincing, provided the attorney could make a plausible explanation?

_____

_____

_____

_____

_____

_____

_____

_____

_____

Study Guide Questions

Multiple Choice

1. *Case law* is another term for this.
a. tort law
b. Hammurabic law
c. statutory law
d. common law

2. These proscribe criminal behavior.
a. the first 10 Constitutional amendments
b. statutes
c. administrative rules
d. procedural law

3. A case is between an individual and the government in this type of law.
a. criminal
b. civil
c. tort
d. common

4. This document dictated protections from the English government.
a. the Treaty of Versailles
b. the Bill of Rights
c. the Magna Carta
d. the U.S. Constitution

5. Substantive law covers this offense.
a. search without a warrant
b. an arrestee is not informed of his/her rights
c. assault
d. an illegal seizure

6. Common law is based on this doctrine.
a. precedent
b. Monroe
c. manifest destiny
d. fairness

7. Community service is a likely punishment for an offender who has committed one of these.
a. a murder
b. a felony
c. a misdemeanor
d. an inchoate offense

8. *Mens rea* refers to this.
a. criminal intent
b. criminal act
c. concurrence
d. *corpus delicti*

9. Felons are not allowed to do this.
a. run for public office
b. have children
c. leave the country
d. leave the state

10. Courts are bound by the decisions of previous courts in a legal principle known as
a. *mea culpa.*
b. *voir dire.*
c. *lex talionis.*
d. *stare decisis.*

True/False

1. Parole agencies may not enact rules limiting the freedom of parolees. _____

2. A defendant who loses a civil case may go to prison. _____

3. Cases decided in one judicial circuit are not necessarily influential in all circuits. _____

4. Misdemeanor offenders sometimes receive alternative sentences. _____

5. Common law is not based on the doctrine of precedent. _____

6. The law not only defines socially unacceptable behaviors, it also regulates how behavior is punished. _____

7. The Bill of Rights specifies the freedoms of U.S citizens. _____

8. Tort law is a form of criminal law. _____

9. Statutes are published in penal codes. _____

10. The Code of Hammurabi is a quite recent development in the law. _____

Fill in the Blank

1. _____ specifies how the criminal justice system may deal with defendants and offenders.

2. Case law is greatly influenced by the issue of _____.

3. _____ requires judges to consider how previous cases have dealt with similar issues.

4. The Bill of Rights is the first 10 _____ to the Constitution.

5. The existence of other means to protect society against undesirable behavior is one of the criteria that determines what behaviors are made _____.

6. Conspiracy is an example of an _____ offense.

7. _____ is the principle that states that a person cannot be tried for the same crime twice.

8. *Actus reus*, *mens rea*, and _____ must be present in order for an act to be considered a crime.

9. The legal term for "body of the crime" is _____.

Find a Flash

Read the two news flashes in Chapter 4 carefully, noting how they illustrate issues covered in the chapter.

- *No Pass for* Murder explains that no statute of limitations exists for murder and reviews how the criminal justice system dealt with the legal issues inherent in prosecuting a 39-year-old man for a murder committed when he was 15.
- *Rodney King and Double Jeopardy* examines the concept of double jeopardy and how it applied to the Los Angeles police officers who were tried twice for beating motorist Rodney King.

Use the library or search the web to find two news items that exemplify, explain, or even appear to contradict topics from Chapter 4. Write short summaries of these news items in the spaces provided. If possible, find one local story and one national story. Give your news flashes short titles that explain what they are about. Suggested news flash topics are listed below.

Constitutions
Statutes
Administrative rules
Criminal law
Civil law
Substantive law
Procedural law
Case law
Felonies
Misdemeanors
Inchoate offenses
Criminal responsibility and criminal defense

News Flash #1

Title

News Flash #2

Title

What Agency Am I?

Peruse the following descriptions taken from the websites of federal criminal justice-related agencies, programs, and bureaus. Find the organization that matches it in the list and write it in the blank space provided. Hint: Use the web addresses in the list to check the organizations' websites.

A. I am the office of the chief law enforcement officer of the federal government. This law enforcement officer represents the United States in general legal matters and advises the president and heads of executive government departments when requested. He or she also represents the government before the U.S. Supreme Court in cases of exceptional gravity or importance.

Who Am I? _____

B. My attorneys serve as the nation's principal litigators under the direction of the attorney general. There are 93 United States Attorneys stationed throughout the United States, Puerto Rico, the Virgin Islands, Guam, and the Northern Mariana Islands. The attorneys prosecute criminal cases brought by the federal government; prosecute and defend civil cases in which the United States is a party; and collect debts owed the federal government.

Who Am I? _____

C. I represent the United States, its departments and agencies, members of Congress, cabinet officers, and other federal employees. My litigation involves the defense of challenges to presidential actions; national security issues; benefit programs; energy policies; commercial issues such as contract disputes, banking insurance, patents, fraud, and debt collection; all manner of accident and liability claims; and criminal violations of the immigration and consumer protection laws. I confront significant policy issues, which often rise to constitutional dimensions, in defending and enforcing various federal programs and actions.

Who Am I?_____

List

Department of Justice Civil Division	http://www.usdoj.gov/civil
Federal Trade Commission	http://www.ftc.gov
National Criminal Justice Reference Service	http://www.ncjrs.org
National Institute of Justice	http://www.ojp.usdoj.gov/nij
Office of the Attorney General	http://www.usdoj.gov/ag
Uniform Crime Reports (FBI)	http://www.fbi.gov/ucr/ucr.htm
United States Attorneys	http://www.usdoj.gov/usao

Word Search

Instructions: Fill in the blanks of the definitions below with the correct word, then find the word in the puzzle!

```
I O B W V R G O E M F Y K Q V A P T A L R N U G O R J W L L
U L B S M X G Y C D O U B L E J E O P A R D Y F Y O Z K X N
T C O D E O F H A M M U R A B I D V G K Q M Z L P U E R T I
O D N U A G B S B Y E J Q U O G S Y I W C A J H A V L Y A C
R Q D Q B U M P M J N P I A U I F I O S S T D S Z K O Q A E
T A I T B K S D B Y E I S E O B T C M C N A J A P V J F Y K
L I J S I D N A P N X C C T S V A L I B I O L L T B T X L S
A G L J O D V T A S N N N U H P C C Y E G A X W U F X R E J
W U H M S D I L N F E V P J W G R G O Q B V E U W Y X G C A
Z M I F X O C V E R P R J G B Z I V V R K C M R S A T C M P
K K P C Z O U L R E O I M U I C Y R T S P S F I S Y A Q T M
X Q X Q D G T U C C T P L M Y N X M F J R U N G T N H H O F
X U E E B V C Q S C N S X X E N C R F O J X S B P N E X Z K
V P Y L T N S A F E I O V L O M D H A Y L B V D L Q C M Z D
P R Y M O O E M A F A V T F U Q T U O U A L B E E U Z J B B
I E E C A B Y R V K J M I J Q R N V I A C T I V N L Y Y P V
N C Q X A I N Q O C C F P L A U Q B J W T H R B W D I K T G
S E E H L L S C H U S X J S L P X D G Q O E L A W U B C L W
A D T S V V E W D W T E N K E A I Y I K Z Z O M C C D K T P
N E S C M R S D U I A K C Q U W W O E T C U F F T A G D Q I
I N X U M G O F F Q R W A P S G T X O S O C B N F S N F H U
T T C G A K O G B Q E T A T Z T C F O B M M I Y Z E P G G Z
Y A E Y C N A F N I D L D C O M G C B D M M S N W C N Q A L
D D K S Y Y E X I L E N Y O T O N H X I O B U F O U K S S M
E O B J F O U R O O C A G R I U D T W T N B O K Y S A Z E I
F S O Y B Y R F V Q I K J B I I S N H T L J V X U U C F P Q
E M T O S D O E Y O S M N R M K P R V I A R E H P P J J D R
N B M O N L V X S F I E T U T A T S E X W Y J V O R R T L X
S V Z I Y P B U N H S Y O U D R K A B U E W O U O E A I S G
E D R J X L V M E J V L Q P U M P G D N S F W T F S N V U W
```

Definitions

1. _____ means "guilty deed."

2. An _____ is a defense that involves the defendant(s) claiming not to have been at the scene of a crime when that crime was committed.

3. The first 10 amendments to the U.S. Constitution are the _____.

4. _____ refers to the law that governs private rights as opposed to the law that governs criminal issues.

5. The _____ is an ancient code instituted by a ruler of Babylonia.

6. _____ is sometimes called case law, judiciary law, judge-made law, customary law, or unwritten law.

7. _____ is the coexistence of *actus reus* and *mens rea*.

8. _____ means "body of the crime."

9. _____ refers to multiple punishments for a single offense.

10. A writ issued to bring a party before the court is called a _____.

11. An offense comprising acts necessary to commit another crime is an _____.

12. Almost all states end _____ at the age of 18.

13. The _____ attempts to give physical or psychological reasons that a defendant cannot comprehend his/her criminal actions, their harm(s), or their punishment.

14. The _____ was a guarantee of liberties signed by King John of England in 1215.

15. _____ refers to intent or knowledge to commit a crime.

16. _____ is a code of laws that deals with crimes and the punishments for them.

17. A prior legal decision used as a basis for deciding a later, similar case is called _____.

18. _____ is the doctrine under which courts adhere to legal precedent.

19. A _____ is a law enacted by a legislature.

20. _____ includes libel, slander, assault, trespass, and negligence.

Match the Case

Part One
Crime: Problems, Measurement, Theories, and Law

Draw a line from the case to its outcome.

Escobedo v. Illinois — Illegally seized evidence is inadmissible in state criminal courts.

People v. Aphaylath — The Supreme Court created a new test for insanity.

Robinson v. California — The value of expert testimony that provides evidence of a pertinent issue is not dependent on whether the witness personally knows a defendant or a defendant's particular characteristics.

Durham v. United States — The Supreme Court holds that drug addiction is a disease, not a crime.

Gideon v. Wainwright — Upon being accused of murder, a suspect is entitled to counsel and the right to remain silent.

Mapp v. Ohio — Indigent defendants have the right to court-appointed attorneys in felony cases.

Chapter 5
History and Organization of Law Enforcement

Learning Objectives
After reading this chapter, students should be able to:

1. Understand how the history of policing can be traced to England.
2. Appreciate how the English heritage of policing produced three enduring features of American policing: limited police authority, local control, and a fragmented system.
3. Discuss how vigilante committees usurped policing in the rural south and west.
4. List several of the features of American policing that led to the professionalization of law enforcement.
5. Identify and explain how the different levels of law enforcement are problematic to policing in the United States.
6. Discuss how programs and research studies such as the Kansas City Preventive Patrol Experiment, the Rand Study of Detectives, and the DARE program have impacted the practice of law enforcement in the United States.
7. Compare and contrast alternative styles of policing such as community policing, problem-oriented policing, and zero-tolerance policing.

Chapter Summary and Key Concepts
Chapter 5 highlights the history of law enforcement and links that history to the way that police agencies are organized today.

History and Development of the Police
- The institution of the police is a relatively new phenomenon, although police have existed in one form or another for thousands of years.
- Police in early history usually derived from the military.
- The development of law enforcement as an institution has been episodic, uneven, and fraught with issues of politics, class and racial biases, and a lack of consensus as to what the police are supposed to do.
- U.S. law enforcement is based on the English system, especially in terms of limited police authority, local control, and a fragmented system.
- In the southern and western United States, vigilante movements provided some social control in areas that lacked established and effective law enforcement agencies.
- Informal policing began in New York City in 1625. Chicago's official police force was created around 1855 and reorganized several times until 1913. Police officers in both cities had broad discretion in enforcement of the law.
- In the 19th century, some companies maintained their own police forces. Two of the most famous are Pennsylvania's Coal and Iron Police and the Pinkerton National Detective Agency.
- The Pendleton Civil Service Act of 1883 formed a civil service system that administered employment and promotions based on merit rather than political connections.

- In 1931, August Vollmer wrote the Wickersham Commission report. Vollmer advocated that police be non-partisan, use scientific principles, become more specialized, and be led by qualified executives who could run large organizations.

Policing Today
- The police are vested with the responsibility of detecting crime and bringing lawbreakers to justice.
- All modern U.S. police departments are organized in a similar fashion.
- The majority of law enforcement agencies are based on a quasi-military template, with uniforms, ranks, hierarchical chains-of-command, and centralized decision-making.
- Although some obvious similarities exist between civilian police and military organizations, individual police officers have more discretion, higher visibility, and a great deal less authority.
- Law enforcement agencies are spread across federal, state, and local levels of administration.

Levels of Law Enforcement
- Federal law enforcement agencies have nationwide jurisdiction but concentrate on specific crimes. The FBI and Secret Service are two examples of federal law enforcement agencies.
- State-level law enforcement is organized in a variety of ways, with each state having a slightly different system. Highway patrol units are the most well-known of the state agencies.
- Local law enforcement agencies handle most of the nation's crime. There are about 13,000 local police departments in the United States.
- Sheriffs' offices are the most common form of county law enforcement in the United States, with about 3,000 offices.

Innovations in Policing
- In 1972, the Kansas City Preventive Patrol Experiment measured the efficacy of police patrol in terms of its effect on crime, the delivery of police services, and citizens' feelings of security. The study found that the level of patrol made little difference.
- In 1977, the Rand Study of Detectives attempted to determine how effective detectives are in solving crimes. The study suggested that more efficient ways may exist for law enforcement agencies to do detective work.
- The Drug Abuse Resistance Education program began in 1983 in Los Angeles to give children information about illegal drugs, what happens when people use or sell illegal drugs, and methods to avoid illegal drugs. Schools throughout the nation are currently running the program.

Key Terms

authority
The right and the power to commit an act or order others to commit an act. Permission.

bobbies
A popular slang term for the police force created in 1829 by Sir Robert Peel's Metropolitan Police Act. The term is derived from the short form of Robert, Bob.

Bow Street Runners
A police organization created circa 1748 by magistrates Henry Fielding and his brother Sir John Fielding whose members went on patrol, rather than sitting at a designated post.

constable
The head of law enforcement for large districts in early England. Constables oversaw the watch-and-ward system that guarded the city's or town's gates at night. In the modern United States, a constable serves areas such as rural townships and is usually elected. The constable is responsible for serving summonses, subpoenas, and court orders.

frankpledge system
Form of English government that began in Anglo-Saxon England and endured until the 19th century. This system divided a community into groups of 10 men (tithings) who were responsible for the conduct of the group and ensured that a member charged with breaking the law would appear in court.

hue and cry
In early English law, the alarm that citizens were require to raise upon the witness or discovery of a crime. The witness and all within earshot were required by law to pursue the perpetrator.

hundred-man
The head of a group of 10 tithings (men collected in groups of 10) who served as an administrator and judge.

Metropolitan Police Act
Created in 1829 by Sir Robert Peel, it was the first successful bill to create a permanent, public police force.

shire reeve
Sheriff. The shire reeve led the shire's military forces and judged cases. Later, sheriff duties were restricted to trying minor crimes, investigating crimes within the shire, and questioning suspects.

Thames River Police
A private police force created by the West India Trading Company in 1798 that represented the first professional, salaried police force in London.

watch-and-ward system
Old English system overseen by the constable in which a watchman guarded a city's or town's gates at night.

Short Answer Questions

Discuss the development of the police force in London. Besides preventing crime, what were the duties of this early police? Why were they called "bobbies"?

_____
_____
_____
_____
_____
_____
_____
_____
_____

What are vigilantes? Describe how they maintained social control in the past. Are there any justifications for this type of behavior in current times? Can you envision any case where you might employ vigilantism?

_____
_____
_____
_____
_____
_____
_____
_____

At what levels of government do we find law enforcement organizations? Why are there different levels of jurisdiction? Why not make one big federal police force responsible for dealing with all crimes?

What was learned from the Kansas City Preventive Patrol Experiment? Are there good reasons for police to patrol the streets or is it just good for public relations?

Has the DARE program worked? Are the police the best agency to provide drug education and drug prevention programs? Is DARE a good program even if it can be shown that it doesn't meet its goals?

_____
_____
_____
_____
_____
_____
_____
_____
_____

Study Guide Questions

Multiple Choice

1. The Thames River police were created by the
   a. English government.
   b. East India Trading Company.
   c. West India Trading Company.
   d. Magna Carta.

2. What did English policing contribute to American policing?
   a. uniforms
   b. guns
   c. foot patrols
   d. limited authority

3. "The swift angel of death" was August Vollmer's term for what?
   a. the patrol car
   b. the radio
   c. the telephone
   d. the hearse

4. In early England, this was a group of 10 men who ensured that a group member who broke the law would go to court.
a. a hundred-man
b. a tithing
c. a frankpledge
d. a deciman

5. The early Chicago police had four idiosyncratic orientations to the law. Which is not one of them?
a. The city criminal justice system emphasized strict legal procedure.
b. Officers developed informal systems of operation that reflected their own subcultures.
c. The police were a significant resource commanded by local organizations.
d. Police and courts were highly decentralized.

6. August Vollmer's police reform movement focused on six issues. Which is not one of them?
a. Policing should be free of political influence.
b. Qualified executives should lead the police.
c. Police should be uniformed.
d. Officers should be screened for intelligence, health, and moral character.

7. Henry and John Fielding developed the
a. watch-and-ward system.
b. FBI.
c. Bobbies.
d. Bow Street Runners.

8. These three differences make supervising the police much different than supervising the military.
a. discretion, visibility, and authority
b. discretion, visibility, and communication
c. organization, weaponry, and authority
d. discretion, weaponry, and authority

9. This U.S. act formed a civil-service system that eliminated patronage and administered employment and promotions based on merit.
a. the Metropolitan Police Act
b. the Pendleton Civil Service Act
c. the Patriot Act
d. the Omnibus Crime Control and Safe Streets Act

10. This was the first successful bill to create a permanent, public police force.
a. the Omnibus Crime Control and Safe Streets Act
b. the Pendleton Civil Service Act
c. the Metropolitan Police Act
d. the Magna Carta

True/False

1. English policing contributed the tradition of limited police authority to U.S. policing. _____

2. The police are like the military primarily in discretion, visibility, and authority. _____

3. There is little variation in the organization of police departments. _____

4. The method of U.S. law enforcement is completely uniform. _____

5. Federal law enforcement agencies have nationwide jurisdiction and pursue all offenses. _____

6. The institution of the police is fairly recent. _____

7. State law enforcement agencies do not have as many officers as local agencies, nor the visibility of federal agencies. _____

8. The Secret Service has many duties. _____

9. The frankpledge system is still in use in England today. _____

10. Vollmer's police reform movement focused on six issues, one of which was that policing should be free of political influence. _____

Fill in the Blank

1. _____ organized the Bow Street Runners to combat an increase in crime.

2. *Miranda v. Arizona* set forth that confessions made by suspects who have not been advised of their _____ cannot be used as evidence.

3. Informal policing began in _____ in 1625 when it was called New Amsterdam.

4. Reformer _____ made the police more efficient by assigning officers based on the amount of reported crime and calls for service.

5. Founded in 1870, the _____ enforces federal laws.

6. Investigating some types of computer fraud is one of the duties of the _____.

7. In the early, rural U.S., especially the south and west, _____ committees were established to protect people and property.

8. Established in 1789, the _____ primarily enforces the collection of revenue.

9. The most common form of _____ law enforcement is sheriffs' offices.

10. _____ built the FBI into one of the premier law enforcement agencies in the world.

Find a Flash
Read the news flash in Chapter 5 carefully, noting how it illustrates issues covered in the chapter.

- *Candid Cop Cameras* describes how Los Angeles police installed motion-sensor cameras in neglected alleys to take photographs of loiterers that may be used in court.

Use the library or search the web to find two news items that exemplify, explain, or even appear to contradict topics from Chapter 5. Write short summaries of these news items in the spaces provided. If possible, find one local story and one national story. Give your news flashes short titles that explain what they are about. Suggested news flash topics are listed below.

Federal-level law enforcement
State-level law enforcement
Local-level law enforcement
State highway patrols
Sheriffs' offices
The FBI
The Secret Service
Innovations in policing
The DARE program
Police jurisdiction
Law enforcement careers

News Flash #1

Title

News Flash #2

Title

What Agency Am I?

Peruse the following descriptions taken from the websites of federal criminal justice-related agencies, programs, and bureaus. Find the organization that matches it in the list and write it in the blank space provided. Hint: Use the web addresses in the list to check the organizations' websites.

A. Since 1789, my law enforcement officers have served the nation through a variety of vital law enforcement activities. Ninety-five officers, appointed by the president or the U.S. attorney general, direct the activities of 94 district offices and personnel at more than 350 locations throughout the 50 states, Guam, Northern Mariana Islands, Puerto Rico, and the Virgin Islands. My responsibilities include judicial security, fugitive investigations, and witness security.

Who Am I? _____

B. Founded by Benjamin Franklin, I am a federal law enforcement agency that protects the U.S. Postal Service, its employees, and its customers from criminal attack, and protects the nation's mail system from criminal misuse.

Who Am I? _____

C. I manage public lands in national forests and grasslands. My mission includes protecting and managing natural resources on National Forest System lands. I also assist state and local governments, forest industries, and private landowners in protecting and managing non-federal forest and associated range and watershed lands.

Who Am I? _____

D. I am a Treasury Department police agency that is responsible for protecting over $100 billion in Treasury and other government assets stored in facilities in Philadelphia; San Francisco; Denver; West Point, New York; Fort Knox, Kentucky; and Washington, D.C. My officers protect life and property; prevent, detect, and investigate criminal acts; collect and preserve evidence; make arrests; and enforce federal and local laws.

Who Am I? _____

List

Federal Trade Commission	http://www.ftc.gov
National Institute of Justice	http://www.ojp.usdoj.gov/nij
Office of the Attorney General	http://www.usdoj.gov/ag
U.S. Marshals Service	http://www.usdoj.gov/marshals
U.S. Mint Police	http://www.usmint.gov/about_the_mint/mint_police
U.S. Postal Inspection Service	http://www.usps.com/postalinspectors
U.S.D.A. Forest Service	http://www.fs.fed.us

Word Search

Instructions: Fill in the blanks of the definitions below with the correct word, then find the word in the puzzle!

```
X T P D J F W B D V H B X G Y L Y E C U V Q H C Q R M U I N
X H U Z M L M F Z T U G O T N C F N L C O B F Z R R F U X N
B M M C J I J F Z S Y P R B C D R A W D N A H C T A W R F U
S O W Y N N E F E D F S X F G L M J I V Z J R Q L D S A H N
Y S W K Y N B U W R T J G V L V D K Z G E H J S I M N Y Y O
P J Q S Z O L L P Z D P G I O P K M I T B A U S M F E J U J
A D T M T D B X V K U P Z D G A U T Z E Y Z I N A O W R E S
B Y N Z M R Y Z U X U Y O B T K X A K I T O Y V W T X F D A
R W F N Q D E M K Y B U E J T O Y B G V U K S E I B B O B V
V J Y O R B D E Q K O P J K P A M Y S H H U P G I E B I L E
D I R W S G D J T V E I P V W C C V M U I O J N O R Y T Y U
L X C W T N P T C R K S B D X O W G M N S K D B S N W K W Z
E D D B C G O K Y Y U F R A N K P L E D G E S Y S T E M Z V
H P N Y A L F Q V K G N T H H P R O Z R V F O K P C X N U O
W F A S S E L Z B L B O N T J H G C H E M A L Y L Z X D D D
N N E V H H G A Y I E K N E P G I X B D J G N X C G P V I E
I Y U C I R F I Z I Q O E T R W T M O M O U U I N U V T N D
V Q H C R K P L S S B W U K S S Q Y H A U I P D M J V F N T
H J Z X E Y F C C M F N G W V K X D E N S R I R Z D M Q M K
M T H B R Z R Y G V J O F L B A T V Q N R Q A T C L T W Z F
G Y O D E G M P X R G Y K M C U E J H I U P L O D J O R I T
T I D W E V W M B T G E M G R T T F N F Y U A P F R V S C N
H C U H V X G P S U W B Z P U H W A Q H V E L B A T S N O C
S K M V E L C U M B D H N S T O E R Q A V R Y X G R X S E K
V Q P W K Y Y V V J S I Q B J R W I S N H G O O L T U C X M
X E D O O Q H S F X A X H K J I X U R F X K R T A B H B T V
Y W B K V V X K C T J V Q G X T Q K W N K K S A T X S D D M
Y E U D P W N U U K C M W F D Y U G V G E Q O Z Z H Q K X Y
M G Z B L X A S K S C M X S V D A D I U O L I H Q J H P D Z
S V F U F X X P V P O H Q Q C G U Q I B H B C J B V O L A I
```

Definitions

1. _____ is the right and the power to commit an act or order others to commit an act.

2. _____ is a popular slang term for the police force created in 1829 by Sir Robert Peel's Metropolitan Police Act.

3. The _____ were created circa 1748 by magistrates Henry Fielding and his brother Sir John Fielding.

4. In early England, the _____ oversaw a town's watch-and-ward system.

5. The _____ was a form of English government that began in Anglo-Saxon England and endured until the 19th century.

6. In early English law, the _____ was the alarm that citizens were required to raise upon the witness or discovery of a crime.

7. The _____ was the head of a group of a hundred men in early England, who served as an administrator and judge.

8. The _____ led a shire's military forces and judged cases.

9. The _____ was an early English system in which a watchman guarded a city's or town's gates at night.

Chapter 6
Controlling the Police

Learning Objectives
After reading this chapter, students should be able to:

1. Define police discretion and explain why it is important to the understanding of police behavior.
2. Evaluate how the popular expectations of the police may exceed their ability to produce effective law enforcement.
3. Discuss the advantages and disadvantages of the quasi-military nature of contemporary police departments.
4. Identify and discuss James Q. Wilson's styles of policing.
5. Explain and critique some of the pitfalls of the policing subculture.
6. Explain the difference between the Knapp Commission's types of police corruption: meat-eaters and grass-eaters.
7. Discuss the many implications of the Fourth Amendment for controlling the police.

Chapter Summary and Key Concepts
Chapter 6 reviews how the police are constrained in their efforts to keep order, provide services to citizens, and fight crime.

The Nature of the Police
- The police decide which laws to enforce, a process known as *discretion*.
- James Q. Wilson identified three styles of policing: watchman style, legalistic style, and service style.
- The watchman style distinguishes between two mandates of policing: order maintenance and law enforcement.
- The legalistic style exercises little discretion and enforces the law by writing more tickets, making more arrests, and encouraging victims to sign complaints.
- The service style shares characteristics with the other two styles but focuses primarily on service to the community and the citizens.

The Police Subculture
- Jerome Skolnick's term *policeman's working personality* explains how law enforcement officers participate in a police subculture that emphasizes different values from those of mainstream society.
- In 1971, the Knapp Commission issued a report on police corruption in New York City. The report made a distinction between meat-eaters and grass-eaters.
- Historically, illegal gambling, prostitution, prohibition, and other organized crime activities have been major sources of police corruption.

The Fourth Amendment
- The text of the Fourth Amendment is: "The right of the people to be secure in their persons, houses, papers, and effects, against unreasonable searches and seizures, shall not be violated, and no Warrants shall issue, but upon probable cause, supported by Oath or affirmation, and particularly describing the place to be searched, and the persons or things to be seized."
- Procedural law controlling the activities of law enforcement is derived from the Fourth Amendment, which specifies a wide range of protections from police activity.
- The court is concerned with several aspects of searches: the trespass doctrine, the privacy doctrine, the plain-view doctrine, the open-fields doctrine, public places, and abandoned property.
- Police must have a warrant to conduct a search, with four major exceptions: searches incident to arrest, consent searches, exigent circumstances searches or emergency searches, and vehicle searches.
- Special-needs searches also do not require warrants. These are inventory searches, border searches, airport searches, searches of prisoners, searches of probationers and parolees, searches of students, and employee drug testing.
- The police cannot present illegally seized evidence in court.
- Stop-and-frisk encompasses two distinct behaviors. Stops may be considered seizures and frisks as searches. For a frisk to be lawful, the stop must meet the conditions of a lawful seizure.
- An arrest involves being taken into custody, photographed, fingerprinted, interrogated, and booked.
- The court recommends four restrictions to arrest someone at their home: the crime should be a felony, the police must knock and announce, the arrest should be made in daylight, and the police must meet a stringent probable-cause requirement.
- Individual rights during interrogations stem from the Fifth Amendment self-incrimination clause, the Sixth Amendment right-to-counsel clause, and the Fourteenth Amendment due-process clause.

Key Terms

actual-seizure stop
Incident in which police officers physically restrain a person and restrict his/her freedom.

grabbable area
The area under the control of an individual during an arrest in an automobile. For example, the inside of the passenger compartment is considered "grabbable area," but not the space under the hood or in the trunk.

grass-eaters
A slang term from the 1971 Knapp Commission report on police corruption in New York City describing officers who accept bribes but do not actively pursue them.

legalistic style
A mode of policing that emphasizes enforcement of the letter of the law. The legalistic officer will write more tickets, make more arrests, and encourage victims to sign complaints. Using little personal discretion, the legalistic officer will make arrests and allow the courts to resolve the incidents.

meat-eaters
A slang term from the 1971 Knapp Commission report on police corruption in New York City describing officers who actively seek out situations that can produce financial gain.

policeman's working personality
A term coined by Jerome Skolnick to refer to the mindset of police who must deal with danger, authority, isolation, and suspicion while appearing to be efficient. Officers may be drawn into a police subculture that emphasizes a different set of values from mainstream society.

probable cause
A reason based upon known facts to think that a crime has taken place or that a property is connected to a crime. A law enforcement officer must have probable cause in order to make an arrest without a warrant, to search without a warrant, or to seize property that may provide evidence of a crime.

racial profiling
Suspicion of illegal activity based on a person's race, ethnicity, or national origin rather than on actual illegal activity or evidence of illegal activity.

reasonable stop standard
Supreme Court measure that considers constitutionality on whether a reasonable person would feel free to terminate an encounter with law enforcement.

reasonable suspicion
A suspicion based on facts or circumstances that justifies stopping and sometimes searching an individual thought to be involved in criminal activity.

seizure
When law enforcement officers take potential evidence in a criminal case. Evidence seized without a search warrant or without probable cause may not be admitted in court.

service style
A mode of policing that is concerned primarily with serving the community and citizens. The service-style officer will use discretion, as with the watchman style, but that discretion is visible, subject to formal review and evaluation, and can be altered when circumstances require.

show-of-authority stop
Incident in which police show a sign of authority (such as flashing a badge), and the suspect submits.

stop
A temporary detention that legally is a seizure of an individual and must be based on reasonable suspicion.

stop-and-frisk
A term that describes two distinct behaviors on the part of law enforcement officers in dealing with suspects. In order to conduct a lawful frisk, the stop itself must meet the legal conditions of a seizure. A frisk constitutes a search.

watchman style
A mode of policing that emphasizes the maintenance of order, rather than law enforcement. Law enforcement emphasizes discovering crimes and offenders and making arrests. Order-maintenance-style policing may tolerate some illegal activity, as long as order is maintained. Discretion is a major part of the officer's job.

Short Answer Questions

Why is police discretion such an important concern? Shouldn't we allow the police to make any decisions they deem appropriate because they risk their lives? Can't we trust the individual law enforcement officer to do the right thing?

_____

_____

_____

_____

_____

_____

_____

_____

_____

_____

_____

_____

What do we mean when we say that the police have an occupational subculture? What are the assumptions of this subculture and how is it related to the use of force?

What are the three styles of policing according to James Q. Wilson? Is any one of the styles superior to the others? Which style of policing would you most likely employ if you were a law enforcement officer?

The Knapp Commission categorized corrupt police offices as "grass-eaters" and "meat-eaters." What do these terms refer to, and which is the more serious? Is there room in a police department for either type of corruption?

What are special-needs searches? Are they simply loopholes in the Fourth Amendment? Should any of them be prohibited?

Study Guide Questions

Multiple Choice

1. Constitutional protection from illegal searches and seizures is provided by the
a. Fourth Amendment
b. Eighth Amendment
c. First Amendment
d. Twenty-third Amendment

2. This case established that police have the right to search suspects to ensure their own safety if they think the suspects are armed.
a. *Katz v. United States*
b. *In re Gault*
c. *Mapp v. Ohio*
d. *Terry v. Ohio*

3. Which is not one of James Q. Wilson's three styles of policing?
a. watchman
b. judicial
c. legalistic
d. service

4. What other way may search-and-seizure be defined?
a. grab-and-run
b. stop-and-frisk
c. stop-and-search
d. seize-and-detain

5. In the 1970s, the Knapp Commission issued a report on this police issue in this city.
a. stress; Los Angeles
b. use of force; Atlanta
c. bureaucracy; Chicago
d. corruption; New York City

6. One of the four restrictions on police when they arrest a suspect in this place is that they must knock-and-announce.
a. at home
b. in a public building
c. in a car
d. in an open field

7. The privacy doctrine, based on this case, holds that people, not places, are protected from government intrusion whenever they have a reasonable expectation of privacy.
a. *Miranda v. Arizona*
b. *Katz v. United States*

c. *Argersinger v. Hamlin*
d. *Terry v. Ohio*

8. The police use this power to decide whether or not to fully enforce the law in a given situation.
a. search-and-seizure
b. duty to arrest
c. discretion
d. force

9. The structure of law enforcement agencies is similar to that of these things.
a. military units
b. prisons
c. corporations
d. gangs

10. This term coined by Jerome Skolnick explains how law enforcement officers participate in an occupational subculture that emphasizes its own values.
a. police stress
b. discretion
c. policeman's working personality
d. solidarity

True/False

1. The Fourth Amendment extends to abandoned property. _____

2. A legalistic police officer does not treat all citizens equally and must use a lot of discretion. _____

3. In service-style policing, discretion is subject to formal review and evaluation. _____

4. Evidence that the police acquire by illegal seizures may be presented in court, according to the Fourth Amendment. _____

5. Most arrests of adults require the police to use force. _____

6. The occupational culture of the police fosters certain personality characteristics in officers. _____

7. Procedural law specifying the activities of law enforcement is derived from the Second Amendment. _____

8. An officer using the watchman style follows the law exactly, even for very minor offenses. _____

9. Most searches require a warrant. _____

10. The police do not make an arrest every time they are legally authorized to do so. _____

Fill in the Blank

1. According to the Knapp Commission report, an officer who _____ is a grass-eater.

2. Danger, authority, symbolic assailants, and social isolation help to construct the _____.

3. The _____ doctrine holds that the detection of evidence by police officers who are merely observing a situation does not constitute a search.

4. The legalistic style of policing requires relatively little _____.

5. The _____ states, "The right of the people to be secure in their persons, houses, papers, and effects, against unreasonable searches and seizures, shall not be violated..."

6. The Constitution does not state that the government cannot search but only that it cannot conduct _____ searches.

7. The _____ style of policing focuses on serving the community.

8. According to the case _____, police have the right to search suspects in order to ensure their own safety if they think that the suspects are armed.

9. A law enforcement officer must obtain the approval of a judge to get a _____.

10. The _____ style of policing distinguishes between two mandates of policing: order maintenance and law enforcement.

Find a Flash
Read the three news flashes in Chapter 6 carefully, noting how they illustrate issues covered in the chapter.

- *Police Indiscretion* describes a 2002 incident in which Houston police were ordered to arrest 278 people in a local area regardless of what they were doing.
- *Seized Assets* details an incident in which a police officer was accused of stealing money under the guise of asset forfeiture.
- *Watch Your Car* reviews the "Watch Your Car" program in which motorists may place stickers on their cars allowing police to pull the car over without cause between the hours of 1 a.m. and 5 a.m.

Use the library or search the web to find two news items that exemplify, explain, or even appear to contradict topics from Chapter 6. Write short summaries of these news items in the spaces provided. If possible, find one local story and one national story. Give your news flashes short titles that explain what they are about. Suggested news flash topics are listed below.

Police discretion
Styles of policing
Police subculture
Police corruption
The Fourth Amendment
Searches
Special-needs searches
Seizures
Stop and frisk
Arrests
Interrogation
Confessions
The exclusionary rule

News Flash #1

Title

News Flash #2

Title

What Agency Am I?

Peruse the following descriptions taken from the websites of federal criminal justice-related agencies, programs, and bureaus. Find the organization that matches it in the list and write it in the blank space provided. Hint: Use the web addresses in the list to check the organizations' websites.

A. I am a Justice Department program that assists state and local law enforcement agencies in increasing the number of officers with advanced education and training assigned to community patrol. I offer federal scholarships to college students who agree to serve where needed on community patrol for at least four years.

Who Am I? _____

B. I am a component of the Department of Homeland Security that provides training, funds for the purchase of equipment, support for the planning and execution of exercises, technical assistance, and other support to assist states and local jurisdictions to prevent, respond to, and recover from acts of terrorism.

Who Am I? _____

C. Formerly part of the Treasury Department, I am now a Department of Homeland Security agency that carries out two significant missions: protection and criminal investigations. I protect the president and vice president, their families, heads of state, and other designated individuals; investigate threats against these protectees; and protect the White House, vice president's residence, foreign missions, and other buildings within Washington, D.C. I also investigate violations of laws relating to counterfeiting of obligations and securities of the United States and financial crimes that include access device fraud, financial institution fraud, identity theft, computer fraud, and computer-based attacks on U.S. financial, banking, and telecommunications infrastructure.

Who Am I?_____

D. I am an Immigration and Customs Enforcement police agency that provides law enforcement and security services to the tenants and daily visitors to all federally owned and leased facilities. I focus on the interior security of the nation and the reduction of crimes and potential threats to federal facilities throughout the nation.

Who Am I?_____

List

Federal Protective Service   http://www.ice.gov/graphics/fps
Office for Domestic Preparedness   http://www.ojp.usdoj.gov/odp
Office of the Police Corps   http://www.ojp.usdoj.gov/opclee
U.S. Marshals Service   http://www.usdoj.gov/marshals
U.S. Secret Service   http://www.ustreas.gov/usss

Word Search

Instructions: Fill in the blanks of the definitions below with the correct word, then find the word in the puzzle!

```
E B C L G H A S P S R E T A E S S A R G P Y I I H I J S S M
G P D G P E H J Y N J F J Y R D C L Z V E R F Z F S H I A Y
C G E M B B B T K U E G S P F G R A B B A B L E A R E A O Z
D D R W E M Z N B J V F M H V G P T K B H L H V O W Y F Y Q
X L G E D Q M H U S I Q E B K X I C Q G A Y R B Q F E Y H R
E G N R K B R N U R F O S U I T V U O O P N E J J F H L O E
K B N I M B J Y P Y S X N P V S D H X S K X I N G Y G B Z I
Y R M T B R K Q R P V S Q T M E A T E A T E R S D E A E R V
J F Z G L V L S T U Z J A L P Z S S M Y O U U Y Q Y O S M T
U N V N I R E W Z Y D L W Q T F D T J O A R D U S U B N A E
W L Z I B W G A R Z H U G Y G D C O J P Q F X F Y X W B A P
R Q H L L A R N I V Z B E C N L D R T U I G V Z H Z R Q E
S F M I F A L R X J J N P K K W I O V C W X C Z A L Q M J P
X I Z F Z Z I N V J Y C Z E Z G B S T O P A N D F R I S K T
O G H O D Q S D F N V B L H Y A S D V W U F Y Q I H Z D F S
F E R R X V T E L S D V S G B N T O Y Z H Q K V V H W P A K
L O V P F B I C V I Q J G L X C W G K M B B B C J F X O R R
D F Q L R H C E S C S Y E U U T Z U Z V K Q A X H I W M Z Z
V Q J A X U X Q I Z D C A O E U W P O H X S C S E I Z U R E
Z I D I G E R X P Z A E P E T Z Y V V E Y B R D T Q O Z I G
O Q O C T D T Y U U L P O T S E R U Z I E S L A U T C A B G
U N V A E U G K S O R Q B E A X U F F O E A N W L Q N K Q Z
G S Q R I Q V E C O G W U K H Q A F X K N J L F Q J F N Z G
B J F G S J A S Z D X Z B J T E G U I V W A J I G O G S M I
B C D K O L T Y F U N K L L Q Q M O P Y I N M L P X Z O E X
I B A L V O S E R V I C E H Q V C C A G M P B H O E T P C P
B H I V P R N Q Q W Z B F E H X J L U F P V D C C K I O D N
Q F F U B Q J E Q N R G B P E W C A B F V O N X J T X V Q G
H D N B G W J N O I C I P S U S E L B A N O S A E R A J D O
W J Y R R T C F N V Y E H Q R I G V T D H D Z Q S C Y W X E
```

Definitions

1. An _____ is an incident in which police officers physically restrain a person and restrict his/her freedom.

2. _____ refers to the area under the control of an individual during an arrest in an automobile.

3. _____ and _____ are slang terms from the 1971 Knapp Commission report on police corruption in New York City that describe officers who accept bribes but do not actively pursue them and those who actively seek out situations that can produce financial gain.

4. _____ is a mode of policing that emphasizes enforcement of the letter of the law.

5. A reason based upon known facts to think that a crime has taken place or that a property is connected to a crime is called _____.

6. Suspicion of illegal activity based on a person's race, ethnicity, or national origin rather than on actual illegal activity or evidence of illegal activity is called _____.

7. A suspicion based on facts or circumstances that justifies stopping and sometimes searching an individual thought to be involved in criminal activity is called _____.

8. When law enforcement officers take potential evidence in a criminal case it is called a _____.

9. _____ is a mode of policing that is concerned primarily with serving the community and citizens.

10. A _____ is a temporary detention that legally is a seizure of an individual and must be based on reasonable suspicion.

11. _____ describes two distinct behaviors on the part of law enforcement officers in dealing with suspects.

12. _____ is a mode of policing that emphasizes the maintenance of order, rather than law enforcement.

Chapter 7
Issues in Policing

Learning Objectives
After reading this chapter, students should be able to:

1. Explain why, and under what circumstances, the use of force is legitimate.
2. Discuss the advantages and issues of using Special Weapons and Tactics (SWAT) teams.
3. Appreciate the special issues that face female police officers.
4. Understand how female offenders and victims present unique problems for law enforcement.
5. Appreciate the special issues faced by minority police officers.
6. Understand how racial profiling is an old practice but a new concern for law enforcement.
7. Describe how community policing differs from traditional police practices.
8. Describe how problem-oriented policing differs from traditional police practices.
9. Explain broken windows theory and discuss why it is problematic.
10. Discuss the special police problems that cause stress.
11. Explain how stress is manifested in police officers and identify the resulting problems.

Chapter Summary and Key Concepts
Chapter 7 reviews several selected critical issues facing law enforcement: use of force, gender and race, challenges to traditional policing, and police stress.

Police Use of Force and Proactive Policing
- According to Egon Bittner, police use of force is limited to certain situations and the performance of official duties, and may not be used maliciously or frivolously.
- The militarization of the police and the war on crime analogy are the most apparent in Special Weapons and Tactics (SWAT) divisions.
- Sometimes police will structure situations to give crime an opportunity to occur, such as prostitution or drug stings.
- Gender and race are important issues in the study of law enforcement.

Challenges to Traditional Policing
- In the past 30 years, three challenges to the traditional policing model have developed: community policing, problem-oriented policing, and zero-tolerance policing.
- Community policing involves citizens in helping to solve law-and-order problems in their communities.
- Problem-oriented policing expands the role of police officer from one of reaction to one of proactive problem-solving.
- Zero-tolerance policing is based on the idea that if all infractions of the law are met with punishment, offenders will refrain from committing more serious crimes.

- The theoretical perspective behind problem-oriented and zero-tolerance policing is called *broken windows*. Broken windows is the idea that untended property or deviant behavior that goes uncorrected or unpunished will attract crime.

Police Stress and Burnout
- Unlike many occupations, physical injury or death is a daily possibility for police officers.
- Issues associated with police stress are alcohol abuse, family problems, and suicide.

Key Terms

broken windows theory
The idea that untended property or deviant behavior will attract crime. This theory is used as a justification for clearing the streets of homeless people, drunks, and unruly teens, even when no crime has been committed.

community policing
A policing strategy that attempts to harness the resources and residents of a given community in stopping crime and maintaining order.

double marginality
A term that refers to the multiple outsider status of women and minority police officers.

Neighborhood Watch
A community policing program that encourages residents to cooperate in providing security for the neighborhood.

problem-oriented policing
A style of policing that attempts to address underlying social problems that contribute to crime.

use of force
The legal police use of violence in order to enforce the law. Excessive use of force is considered police brutality.

zero-tolerance policing
This form of policing punishes every infraction of the law, however minor, with an arrest, fine, or other penalty, with the idea that criminals will refrain from committing more serious crimes.

Short Answer Questions

What are legitimate reasons to use a SWAT team? Are SWAT teams an easy answer to difficult problems or are they absolutely necessary?

Women police officers now serve in many law enforcement agencies. Why did it take women so long to break into this previously all-male occupation? Were there any good reasons to prevent women from being police officers?

What is community-oriented policing? Isn't all policing community policing?

What is the broken windows theory? What are the problems, if any, with this type of social control? Does practical application of the broken windows theory make the community a more desirable place to live?

What are the sources of police stress and burnout? What can be done to make the occupation less damaging to those who must enforce the law? Is being a law enforcement officer worth the stress?

___

Study Guide Questions

Multiple Choice

1. Problem-oriented policing evolved from the
a. strain theory.
b. broken windows theory.
c. Marxist theory.
d. labeling theory.

2. This Supreme Court case set forth that an arrest warrant allows only the search of a suspect's person and the immediate vicinity and that further searches require a search warrant.
a. *Terry v. Ohio*
b. *Miranda v. Arizona*
c. *Chimel v. California*
d. *Tennessee v. Garner*

3. The term "suicide by cop" refers to
a. a police officer committing suicide.
b. a suspect attempting to have an officer kill him/her.

c. an officer interrupting a person's suicide attempt.
d. a suspect who is trying to get arrested.

4. Police agencies and military organizations do this differently.
a. have a chain of command
b. use weapons
c. obey orders
d. make decisions

5. This is a situation that police have structured in order to give crime an opportunity to occur.
a. trap
b. DARE
c. SWAT
d. sting

6. This style of policing recalls the watchman style of policing.
a. community policing
b. legalistic policing
c. service-style policing
d. zero-tolerance policing

7. This style of policing is much like community policing, but is much more proactive.
a. broken windows policing
b. zero-tolerance policing
c. problem-oriented policing
d. legalistic policing

8. This is the theoretical perspective behind zero-tolerance policing.
a. XYY theory
b. control theory
c. labeling theory
d. broken windows theory

9. Mentoring may help alleviate this police problem.
a. stress
b. paperwork
c. long hours
d. understaffing

10. Rescuing officers or citizens endangered by gunfire is a job for
a. firefighters.
b. a SWAT team.
c. the BATF.
d. the Federal Marshals.

True/False

1. The police do not routinely use excessive force. _____

2. Gender and race are important issues in the study of law enforcement. _____

3. Community policing is based on the idea that if every minor infraction of the law is punished, criminals will refrain from committing more serious crimes. _____

4. Broken windows theory influences problem-oriented policing. _____

5. Job stress and the policing subculture are not related to alcohol abuse in police officers. _____

6. Some studies have shown that suicide is an occupational hazard for police officers. _____

7. Police departments usually have no policies to help individual officers. _____

8. Family members of police officers usually do not experience stress. _____

9. Police may use physical force whenever they feel like it. _____

10. The police and the military have much in common. _____

Fill in the Blank

1. _____ involves having citizens help solve crime problems in their communities.

2. _____ is intended to "put more eyes on the street."

3. A common critique of _____ theory is that removing "undesirable" people from a community does not mean that crime problems will disappear.

4. In _____, the Supreme Court ruled that deadly force may only be used if a suspect is a threat to the lives of police officers and/or bystanders.

5. In policing, most discretion is in the hands of the _____.

6. Most police officers are not required to use any _____ at all in their everyday duties.

7. _____ is believed to be an occupational hazard for police officers.

8. Like military organizations, police agencies have a _____ structure.

9. _____ was the first city in which black people served as police officers.

10. Jerome Skolnick coined the term "policeman's working personality" to explain how officers must cope with _____, _____, _____, and _____.

Find a Flash
Read the four news flashes in Chapter 7 carefully, noting how they illustrate issues covered in the chapter.

- *Waco, Texas* reviews the 1993 standoff between members of the Branch Davidian sect and federal law enforcement.
- *Ruby Ridge, Idaho* reviews the 1992 shootout between members of the Weaver family and federal law enforcement.
- *A New Face on Racial Profiling* looks at how the racial-profiling controversy has changed since September 11, 2001, to include people of Middle-Eastern descent, as well as Hispanic/Latino and black citizens.
- *Computers Add New Twist to Police Learning Curve* discusses how law enforcement officers have had to become proficient in computer crime investigation.

Use the library or search the web to find two news items that exemplify, explain, or even appear to contradict topics from Chapter 7. Write short summaries of these news items in the spaces provided. If possible, find one local story and one national story. Give your news flashes short titles that explain what they are about. Suggested news flash topics are listed below.

Police use of force
SWAT teams
Proactive policing
Women as police officers
Minorities as police officers
Community policing
Problem-oriented policing
Zero-tolerance policing
Family problems and the police
Broken windows
Police and alcohol
The police and suicide
Police stress

News Flash #1

Title

News Flash #2

Title

What Agency Am I?

Peruse the following descriptions taken from the websites of federal criminal justice-related agencies, programs, and bureaus. Find the organization that matches it in the list and write it in the blank space provided. Hint: Use the web addresses in the list to check the organizations' websites.

A. I am a Treasury Department agency that supports law enforcement investigative efforts and fosters interagency and global cooperation against domestic and international financial crimes. I also provide policy makers with strategic analyses of domestic and worldwide money laundering developments.

Who Am I? _____

B. Since becoming part of the Department of Homeland Security in 2003, I focus exclusively on immigration and citizenship services.

Who Am I? _____

C. I coordinate, direct, and perform highly specialized activities to protect U.S. information systems and produce foreign intelligence information. One of the most important government centers of foreign language analysis and research, I protect all classified and sensitive information that is stored or sent through U.S. government equipment. I also conduct one of the government's leading research and development programs.

Who Am I?_____

D. Located within the Department of Homeland Security, I manage, control, and protect the nation's borders at and between the official ports of entry.

Who Am I?_____

E. I am a police agency that prevents, detects, and investigates criminal acts and enforces traffic regulations throughout congressional buildings, parks, and thoroughfares. My officers also protect members of Congress, the U.S. Senate, the U.S. House of Representatives, and their families.

Who Am I?_____

List

Financial Crimes Enforcement Network	http://www.fincen.gov
National Institute of Justice	http://www.ojp.usdoj.gov/nij
National Security Agency	http://www.nsa.gov
U.S. Capitol Police	http://www.uscapitolpolice.gov
U.S. Citizenship and Immigration Service	http://uscis.gov
U.S. Customs and Border Protection	http://cbp.gov

Word Search

Instructions: Fill in the blanks of the definitions below with the correct word, then find the word in the puzzle!

```
F Y H G L X Q N P M X U F A Z X Y B P Z Y B D S N E V P R V
D O U B L E M A R G I N A L I T Y J P N A D R E U H C H G Y
J N L F D Y I X J H I R M I M Q H I Y R V E I S X S J R U V
H S K G D K Z T O Z T R S G I B C P Y I Z G P P B R B W I U
D T Q F H D X B X T Y Z Q Q T W H Z B K H G M U K R Q F I U
J R G N U A K X J T B E R X Z Q F K Y B W W O V O I D H C P
J Q S P O J N Z X M B R V Q Y J F D O L M E L K Q I W B Q G
M K O P O J T V U P O C W F T M T R M D W I E Y D L S Z Y E
Z T M C Z I S D L T A E M U B N H R R H X N H Z I J G D V C
U S E O F F O R C E Q P K S P O E E O L W Y U S A M V L P M
G N V S G K C B Z L D P M I O Y B L Q I C B X I O J W U Q O
K X M Q Z S K G K W F G U D T S C E N D A B U M U E R C Z A
Z B Q Y V W E D O Z W S W W U Y V D Z N E K P N C U C C T C
W O G K J P M M L E W A P J H C O F U X X S H N B Y O K O O
H H J R L U N L Y X T W D C O W K D B F O R Q U A W S M O W
E L V O D V B M K C O W E E S J Z W B U J W Y S G J M S T Q
P L F F V M M I H C L F Q T T E S C M J T W K I K U L U N E
V H H K A G C B Q Y P S H R R N L Z U E I Q Y V N B Z D U V
K P W N P J G G D Q L E Q O O W E E E Y F S D I A K E W L O
D N H L H H O C H N O L T X I J I I C Z H H T I T I S E D W
D B O V S M Q A U R Y O Q R V L A L R N O Y T E P K E S K U
R A Z C O T Y E Y R L X T Y O W B W V O P Y A B R S A L R P
G G N D M D D G U E X U L F T O X L M O M U O A L S X I I T
U C S F Z U F U R W B K I O K S P Z L A M E O U W K T S K X
P Q T N U U G A I Y N W D Z C V J I Q M T K L Q Z U L D N T
I G T Z X P N C J J Y M R N H Q C V Q Y K O Y B U U U S T D
W J N Y L C V J O E Y E J F I I H T W F T H T M O X T U P A
L A U M E I N L A Z N M D M N D F W Y E Y U R H D R D I M V
G X E B J Z Y J F X D U Z G U F T J X J P J W P P N P S F C
P T R G S T S K U O R J J B Z M J T M C M Y S V S Q Q O W S
```

Definitions

1. _____ is the idea that untended property or deviant behavior will attract crime.

2. _____ attempts to harness the resources and residents of a given community in stopping crime and maintaining order.

3. _____ refers to the multiple outsider status of women and/or minority police officers.

4. _____ is a community policing program that encourages residents to cooperate in providing security for the neighborhood.

5. _____ policing attempts to address the underlying social problems that contribute to crime.

6. The _____ of policing emphasizes an impersonal and legalistic approach to enforcing the law.

7. _____ refers to legal police use of violence in order to enforce the law.

8. _____ policing punishes every minor infraction of the law.

Match the Case

Part Two
Enforcing the Law

Draw a line from the case to its outcome.

Florida v. Bostick	Deadly force now may only be used if the suspect(s) pose a threat to the lives of police officers or bystanders.
Weeks v. United States	Probable cause for a search does not demand proof beyond a reasonable doubt.
Miranda v. Arizona	Police have the right to search suspects in order to ensure their own safety if they think that the suspects are armed.
Chimel v. California	The test of what constitutes seizure is whether the suspect is free to decline an officer's request for a search and terminate the encounter.
Tennessee v. Garner	An arrest warrant allows only the search of a suspect's person and the immediate vicinity. Any further searches require a search warrant.
Illinois v. Gates	The exclusionary rule, which states that illegally seized evidence is inadmissible in court, is applicable to federal criminal proceedings.
Terry v. Ohio	This decision set forth that confessions made by suspects who have not been advised of their due process rights cannot be used as evidence.

Chapter 8
History and Organization of Courts

Learning Objectives
After reading this chapter, students should be able to:

1. Explain why some observers see U.S. courts as "an institution in crisis."
2. Discuss how courts are subject to outside influences.
3. Outline the history of courts.
4. Discuss trial by ordeal and trial by battle.
5. Discuss the Assize of Clarendon.
6. Discuss the beginnings of the jury trial.
7. Discuss the Magna Carta.
8. Explain the problems of early American courts.
9. Discuss U.S. slave courts.
10. Draw a connection between England's legal treatment of early American colonists and the Revolution.
11. Discuss the cases, historical events, and individuals that have affected the way the courts have evolved.
12. Explain court organization; include the federal court system and courts of appeals.
13. Discuss the role of the Supreme Court.
14. Discuss specialized federal courts and the types of cases they handle.
15. Discuss the role of the judge.

Chapter Summary and Key Concepts
Chapter 8 reviews the history and organization of U.S. courts, including federal and state courts.

The History of the Court
- Underlying the role of the court is the idea that justice should be blind to wealth, power, and social class.
- Courts have been consistent features of many societies and are a result of the increasing sophistication of societies in which a division of labor is necessary.
- Part of the development of courts in Europe stemmed from the practice of collecting compensation from the family of the accused for the family of the victim.
- Gradually, courts were held to resolve disputes in a peaceful manner, and more fees were charged as more behaviors became criminalized and considered as crimes against the government. Courts became an important source of revenue for the nobility.
- The English inquest can be considered to be the first type of jury.
- In 1166, the Assize of Clarendon marked the beginning of the grand jury system.
- The jury trial came about in the early 13th century when the Roman Catholic Church halted trials by ordeal.
- In 1215, the Magna Carta set a precedent of encoding into the law limitations on the state's power.

- The 15th-century Court of the Star Chamber was established to deal with a variety of offenses and became known for its violations of citizens' rights.
- The development of the English courts between the 11th and 18th centuries provided the foundation for U.S. courts.
- Many legal protections that existed for defendants in England were absent in colonial America.
- One of the consequences of independence from England is the documents that were created to specify the relationship between the people and the state, including the Bill of Rights and the Constitution.

Modern U.S. Courts
- Modern U.S. courts determine the guilt or innocence of the defendant and decide the disposition or sentence.
- The court is subject to outside forces. The court does not control how it is financed; it does not control how many cases are sent to it; it cannot ensure adequate resources to carry out its sentences; and because its work is done in a courtroom open to the press, it cannot control its public image.
- Courts are divided into state and federal entities.
- Federal courts comprise magistrate courts, U.S. district courts, U.S. Circuit Courts of Appeal, and the U.S. Supreme Court.
- Federal courts hear cases involving the following issues: the U.S. government or one of its officers is being sued; cases between two or more states; cases involving counsels, ambassadors, and other public ministers; laws enacted by Congress; treaties and laws related to maritime jurisdiction; and commerce on the high seas.
- Specialized federal courts include the Tax Court, the Court of Federal Claims, the Court of Veterans Appeal, the Court of International Trade, and the Court of Appeals for the federal circuit, the U.S. Court of Appeals, and the tribal court.
- State courts are divided into the state trial courts of limited and general jurisdiction, intermediate courts of appeals, and state supreme courts.
- Juvenile courts are part of the state court system, but differ in their goals and in the way they operate.
- The U.S. Supreme Court is at the top of the hierarchical jurisdiction for both the federal and state court system.
- The Supreme Court hears about 80 cases a year, all of which must involve a "substantial federal question."

Jurisdiction
- The term *jurisdiction* refers to the authority of the court to hear certain cases.
- Jurisdiction is dependent on the gravity of the case, the location of the offense, and whether the case is being heard for the first time or is on appeal.
- The three types of jurisdiction are subject matter jurisdiction, geographic jurisdiction, and hierarchical jurisdiction.

Civil Law and Criminal Law
- The major distinction between criminal law and civil law is that violations of criminal law are punishable by imprisonment.
- Criminal law concerns the major violations against society: murder, rape, robbery, theft, etc.
- Civil laws govern private issues, such as breach of contract, probate, divorce, and negligence. Violations of civil law are not punishable by prison.

Key Terms

amicus curiae
Someone who is not a part of a case who gives advice or testimony. Also called "friend of the court."

Assize of Clarendon
A 12th-century English law that established judicial procedure and the grand jury system. It also took power from the local courts and returned it to the English crown.

blood feud
A disagreement, the settlement of which is based on personal vengeance and physical violence.

circuit court
A court that holds sessions at intervals within different areas of a judicial district.

compurgation
In medieval German and English law, a defendant could establish innocence by taking an oath and having a required number of people to swear that they believed the oath. Also called "wager of law." Compurgation was permitted until 1833.

Court of the Star Chamber
An ancient meeting place of the king of England's councilors in the palace of Westminster in London, so called because of stars painted on the ceiling. The court was separate from common law courts. Although its sentences included corporal punishments, convicts were never sentenced to death. It was abolished by the Long Parliament in 1641.

courts of appeals
Intermediate courts that dispose of many appeals before they reach the Supreme Court.

district courts
Courts of general jurisdiction that try felony cases involving federal laws and civil cases involving amounts of money over $75,000.

geographic jurisdiction
This is established when the location of a crime dictates which court will hear a case.

hierarchical jurisdiction
This is established when a case is heard by a court according to where that case is located in the system. For example, trial courts hear the facts of the case, determine guilt or innocence, and impose sentence. Appellate courts review the work of the trial court judge and determine whether the case was handled according to the Constitution.

inquest
In archaic usage, considered to be the first type of jury. The English crown conducted proceedings to determine which lands it had conquered and who owned them. The inquest was eventually broadened to concerns other than land ownership.

lower court
Sometimes called "inferior courts," in reference to their hierarchy. These courts receive their authority and resources from local county or municipal governments.

magistrate court
The lowest level of the federal court system, created in 1968 to ease the caseload of the U.S. District Courts.

rule of four
A rule that states that at least four of the nine Supreme Court justices must vote to hear a case.

state court
A hierarchical system of general courts and special courts funded and run by each state. Each state has a different system.

subject matter jurisdiction
When the nature of the case determines which court hears it. An example would be the distinction between felonies and misdemeanors.

writ of certiorari
An order from a superior court calling up for review the record of a case from a lower court.

U.S. Supreme Court
The "court of last resort." The highest court in the United States, established by Article 3 of the Constitution, hears only appeals, with some exceptions.

Short Answer Questions

How were disputes resolved before courts existed? Did these mechanisms resolve issues effectively?

_____
_____
_____
_____
_____
_____
_____
_____
_____
_____

Explain the history of the development of the jury system. Why were members of the community brought into the legal system?

_____
_____
_____
_____
_____
_____
_____
_____
_____

What are the differences between the federal court system and the state court system? At what points of a case might the two systems intersect?

_____
_____
_____
_____
_____
_____
_____
_____
_____

At what points in a criminal case can the verdict be appealed? Why can a state case be heard in a federal appellate court?

_____
_____
_____
_____
_____
_____
_____
_____
_____

What is the role of the U.S. Supreme Court in the organization of the state and federal court system? What types of cases are brought before the U.S. Supreme Court?

Study Guide Questions

Multiple Choice

1. This early court was infamous for its lack of due process.
   a. common-law court
   b. the U.S. Supreme Court
   c. the Court of the Star Chamber
   d. chancery court

2. Under the Sixth Amendment, defendants charged with serious crimes are entitled to this.
   a. trial by jury
   b. trial by ordeal
   c. bench trial
   d. incarceration

3. This was a series of ordinances that established the beginnings of the grand jury system.
   a. Assize of Clarendon
   b. laws of Hammurabi
   c. Magna Carta
   d. the U.S. Constitution

4. This document placed the English king under the rule of law.
a. the Star Chamber Compact
b. the English Bill of Rights
c. the U.S. Constitution
d. the Magna Carta

5. This is the lowest level of the federal court system.
a. chancery court
b. district court
c. Supreme Court
d. magistrate court

6. What was compurgation?
a. going to trial
b. being burned at the stake
c. engaging in trial by battle
d. taking an oath

7. How many cases per year does the U.S. Supreme Court hear?
a. 20
b. 40
c. 80
d. 200

8. Trial by hot water was a type of trial by
a. fire.
b. ordeal.
c. battle.
d. jury.

9. These kinds of courts are generally divided according to a hierarchy of trial courts, appeals courts, and supreme courts.
a. juvenile courts
b. equity courts
c. state courts
d. common-law courts

10. This is an example of why courts had to be invented.
a. compurgation
b. blood feuds
c. war
d. crime

True/False

1. The U.S. court system is very orderly and easy to understand. _____

2. The Supreme Court can review any case it wishes. _____

3. Appellate courts are responsible for ensuring correct application of substantive law. _____

4. The U.S. criminal court system is not an adversarial process. _____

5. Many societies have courts of some type. _____

6. Juvenile courts operate differently than state criminal courts. _____

7. The jury trial developed in the 13th century because the Roman Catholic church forbade priests to participate in trials by ordeal. _____

8. There was a strict line between civil and criminal cases in medieval courts. _____

9. The major difference between criminal and civil law is that violations of civil law are punishable by imprisonment. _____

10. Trials by ordeal depended on divine intervention to demonstrate the innocence of the accused. _____

Fill in the Blank

1. The _____ established the Supreme Court's power as the final word in all cases.

2. The case _____ provided for the expansion of federal power into areas such as banking and social programs.

3. _____ was the basis for the South's Jim Crow laws.

4. _____ refers to a court's authority to hear certain cases.

5. _____ courts implement substantive law.

6. The case _____ initiated the practice of presenting Supreme Court decisions as collective opinions.

7. The legal, Latin term for "friend of the court" is _____.

8. The four levels of federal courts are _____ courts, U.S. _____ courts, U.S. Circuit Courts of _____, and the U.S. Supreme Court.

9. _____ jurisdiction is determined by the nature of a case.

10. The _____ is considered to be the first type of jury.

Find a Flash
Read the two news flashes in Chapter 8 carefully, noting how they illustrate issues covered in the chapter.

- *So Help Me Who?* reviews an incident in which a juror refused to take an oath that included "so help you God."
- *Capital Trials Are Costly* looks at the expense of the death penalty.

Use the library or search the web to find two news items that exemplify, explain, or even appear to contradict topics from Chapter 8. Write short summaries of these news items in the spaces provided. If possible, find one local story and one national story. Give your news flashes short titles that explain what they are about. Suggested news flash topics are listed below.

Courts in history
The grand jury
The jury trial
Due process
Court organization
Jurisdiction
Federal courts
U.S. Supreme Court
Specialized federal courts
State courts
State supreme courts

News Flash #1

Title

News Flash #2

Title

What Agency Am I?

Peruse the following descriptions taken from the websites of federal criminal justice-related agencies, programs, and bureaus. Find the organization that matches it in the list and write it in the blank space provided. Hint: Use the web addresses in the list to check the organizations' websites.

A. My duty is to enforce the law and defend the interests of the United States according to the law; to ensure public safety against threats foreign and domestic; to provide federal leadership in preventing and controlling crime; to seek just punishment for those guilty of unlawful behavior; to administer and enforce the nation's immigration laws fairly and effectively; and to ensure fair and impartial administration of justice for all Americans.

Who Am I? _____

B. My courts often are called the guardians of the Constitution because their rulings protect rights and liberties guaranteed by the Constitution. Through fair and impartial judgments, my courts interpret and apply the law to resolve disputes. My judges are appointed for life, and they can be removed from office only through impeachment and conviction by Congress of "treason, bribery, or other high crimes and misdemeanors."

Who Am I? _____

C. I was created in accordance with Article III, Section 1, of the Constitution and by authority of the Judiciary Act of September 24, 1789. I was organized on February 2, 1790. I am the highest court within the U.S. court system.

Who Am I? _____

List
Department of Justice	http://www.usdoj.gov
Federal Judiciary	http://www.uscourts.gov
Federal Trade Commission	http://www.ftc.gov
National Institute of Justice	http://www.ojp.usdoj.gov/nij
Office of the Attorney General	http://www.usdoj.gov/ag
U.S. Marshals Service	http://www.usdoj.gov/marshals
U.S. Supreme Court	http://www.supremecourtus.gov

Word Search

Instructions: Fill in the blanks of the definitions below with the correct word, then find the word in the puzzle!

```
H E R N B Q E R D S X O N I R W M K J Y P R E M K U B Q U Z
S L N Z U X W Z A Q P C D J A G L K V P W M V J A F F Q J W
W W I W E A E I N G A U F U B U F G E J E A I K C A R F E K
G L H J G O Y V R A S C I H P A R G O E G G X E I F V Y U S
S S M V P Z G G L Q P Z U M K G F E Z E G I S P E X M L D U
B W T S L J R G M P C N O A H Y N K J A G S B Y X Y B O L K
M I Y X R H T V Y J F I E J Z L W G Z I H T Y F B T H G B G
D K J V I U L O L Y A M Z M S L I D K C H R S D L D O E W T
S Q Z E R J L M B R Z I H U H M G O V V M A R S I N S P V S
P H U G A J N E R T K X Q Q A G D M W X F T T I R A T K B E
F T T S R V B O O K T W V J O C U D Z O Y E Z C C X L J V U
Y R K T O S Q Q I F K X T Q B L E F S P F P I H V I I O V Q
H U Z R I S F K E T F P T F J O F A M I C U S C U R I A E N
I O G U T K T X S C A O Z U F E D N A U V R D B X T A J U I
R C H O R X E H Q C I G U X P Z O G Q H E P G W N X W S G Y
N E T C E A R E S B V N R R E K O N C R K S L X M B H W K U
A M P R C C I R C U I T T U C S L V J I E G J O B G Z Q E F
V E Q E F N V X A V O R V H P I B F X U G N R U S B E K J C
X R U W O D E F E E U W U H U M D M U U H V T Y L V E T H E
U P X O T T Q J F O B C R V M U O O I S N Q U T R B D W W H
K U N L I J F N C G K X P D Y K Z C R E O P C G K J D M D H
X S M S R B C E H R K A K Y W M Z R Z V L W J V Z J D O P B
R S Q N W Z T I H C O U R T S O F A P P E A L S S F Q K J V
J U M P E A B D Z S V W A N R L K D G R L B D H W X R L M T
D Q O R T S U E F I S J E L B Q Q S H C E J B Z S V U F H H
H N Z S A Q A F I J B H T Q Q Y I I G T K M L M S Q T A S V
T V L I O C W H B Z X L X L G K O W I R C W D G C A Z N N A
U Q E Z C F P L L P U Q H L I L A C I H C R A R E I H D P N
D T Q J Z T P M J A L C V J I J M A N L J J J D Q U S E K A
O M X E C M B N J C N E T L L Y Q T V M L W Q U X L H Z F H
```

Definitions

1. _____ means "friend of the court."

2. The settlement of a _____ is based on personal vengeance and physical violence.

3. A _____ court holds sessions at intervals within different areas of a judicial district.

4. Also called "wager of law," _____ was permitted until 1833.

5. _____ are intermediate courts that dispose of many appeals before they reach the Supreme Court.

6. _____ jurisdiction is established when location of a crime dictates which court will hear a case.

7. _____ jurisdiction is established when a case is heard by a court according to where that case is located in the system.

8. In archaic usage, the _____ is considered to be the first type of jury.

9. _____ are sometimes called "inferior courts."

10. _____ court is the lowest level of the federal court system.

11. According to the _____, at least four of the nine Supreme Court justices must vote to hear a case.

12. _____ is a hierarchical system of general courts and special courts funded and run by each state.

13. The _____ is the "court of last resort."

14: A _____ is an order from a superior court calling up for review the record of a case from a lower court.

Chapter 9
Working in the Courtroom

Learning Objectives
After reading this chapter, students should be able to:

1. Understand the concept of the courtroom workgroup.
2. List and describe the various participants in the workgroup.
3. Discuss the role of the prosecutor.
4. Describe the difference between the roles of federal and state prosecutors.
5. Understand how some state prosecution offices have special bureaus and programs.
6. Discuss the role of the defense attorney.
7. Describe the defense attorney's role within the courtroom workgroup.
8. Compare and contrast private attorneys and public defenders.
9. Describe the roles and concerns of defendants, victims, and witnesses.
10. Discuss pretrial release decisions.

Chapter Summary and Key Concepts
Chapter 9 explains how the courts function and what roles are played by those responsible for processing criminal cases.

The Courtroom Work Group
- The *courtroom workgroup* refers to those who work in the courtroom. There is a great deal of cooperation inherent in the daily routine of the court.
- Participants in the courtroom workgroup include the judge, the prosecutor, the defense, victims/defendants/witnesses, law enforcement officers, court support staff, corrections officers, and the public.

The Prosecutor
- The prosecutor acts as a gatekeeper in deciding which cases are inserted into the system and which are dismissed.
- According to David Neubauer, the prosecutor's workload can be categorized into the following: fighting, negotiating, drafting, counseling, and administering.
- The Department of Justice is at the top of the federal prosecution hierarchy.
- Three Justice Department offices affect the prosecutorial aspect of the criminal justice process: the offices of the solicitor general, the Department of Justice Criminal Division, and the U.S. attorneys in the federal courts.
- Three types of prosecutors are typically found in state court systems: the state attorney general, the chief prosecutor, and local prosecutors.
- The state prosecutor is the primary representative of the state in the courtroom.
- In large jurisdictions, the prosecutor's office may be divided into bureaus, special units, and programs that address specific issues within the local criminal justice system.
- State court systems are decentralized, with prosecution responsibility distributed across state, county (or district), and local levels.

The Defense Attorney
- The defense attorney is responsible for protecting the interests of the accused and ensuring that the prosecution has adequately proved the charges.
- While defense attorneys must provide the best defense possible for the defendant, the defense attorney often develops a working relationship with the group.
- Each state has its own system to provide for the defense of indigent clients. These fall into three broad categories: assigned counsel, contract systems, and public defenders.

The Judge
- The term "judge" encompasses a range of responsibilities from the local justice of the peace to a Supreme Court justice.
- Judges act as a check-and-balance to the discretion of prosecutors, an impartial arbiter in the contest between law enforcement and defendants, and a decision-maker in applying punishment or treatment of the guilty.
- The duties and roles of judges include signing search warrants, informing defendants of charges, appointing counsel, setting bail, taking pleas, ruling on motions, participating in or ruling on plea bargains, presiding at trials, and sentencing.
- The three methods of judicial selection are executive appointment, election, and merit selection (also called Missouri Bar Plan). Some states use a combination of these methods.

Defendants, Victims, and Witnesses
- Because defendants, victims, and witnesses are unfamiliar with how the court works, they often find it alienating.
- Many jurisdictions have established victim/witness assistance programs to encourage cooperation in criminal cases.
- Courts have developed several systems to help ensure the defendant's appearance: cash bond, property bond, release on recognizance (ROR), or bail agent.

Pretrial Release Decisions
- The pretrial release decision is an important crossroads in the criminal justice system.
- Systems to ensure that the defendant will appear after release include cash bond, property bond, release on recognizance, and bail agent.
- If concerns about public safety or the defendant's likelihood to show are pronounced, then bail may not be allowed.

Key Terms

bail agent
An employee of a private, for-profit company that provides money for suspects to be released from jail. Bail companies usually charge the suspect a fee of 10 percent of the amount of the bond. Also called a "bondsman."

child advocate
An officer appointed by the court to protect the interests of the child and to act as a liaison between the child, the child's family, the court, and any other agency involved with the child. Some states have child-advocate offices.

clerk of the court
The primary administrative officer of each court who manages non-judicial functions. Among the clerk's duties are maintaining records and dockets, paying all collected monies into the U.S. Treasury, administering the jury, providing interpreters and court reporters, and sending official notices and summons.

court administrator
An officer responsible for mechanical necessities of the court including, but not limited to, scheduling courtrooms, managing case flow, administering personnel, procuring furniture, and preparing budgets.

court reporter
A court officer who records and transcribes an official verbatim record of the legal proceedings of the court.

disposition
The final determination of a case or other matter by a court or other judicial entity. This term can also refer to the sentence received by a convicted criminal defendant.

going rate
A term describing how similar cases have been settled by a given set of judges, prosecutors, and attorneys.

Missouri Bar Plan
A judicial nominating commission presents a list of candidates to the governor, who decides on a candidate. After a year in office, voters decide on whether to retain the judge. Judges must run for such re-election each term. Also called *merit selection*.

Short Answer Questions

What is the courtroom work group? How can we call this a group when its participants come from so many different agencies?

What types of activities does a prosecutor engage in? Which of these activities is the prosecutor best trained for and which is the prosecutor least trained for?

Not all defense attorneys are the same. What issues should you consider when selecting a defense attorney to represent you in a criminal case?

What roles does the judge play in a criminal trial? Who has more power in determining the outcome of a case: the prosecutor or the judge?

How are judges selected? Which is the best way to pick a judge? What are the advantages and disadvantages of electing judges?

_____

_____

_____

_____

_____

_____

_____

_____

_____

Study Guide Questions

Multiple Choice

1. The appeals of cases that went against the federal government in the lower courts are coordinated by this person.
  a. magistrate judge
  b. solicitor general
  c. prosecutor
  d. clerk of court

2. The primary law enforcement officer in a community is the
  a. chief prosecutor.
  b. chief defense attorney.
  c. judge.
  d. clerk of court.

3. These criminal justice system actors defend the United States in civil suits.
  a. U.S. Marshals
  b. solicitors general
  c. U.S. defense attorneys general
  d. U.S. attorneys

4. This court officer prepares transcripts of court proceedings.
a. court reporter
b. judge
c. clerk of the court
d. bailiff

5. In jurisdictions that have these systems, a full-time staff of attorneys represents indigent offenders.
a. public-defender systems
b. assigned counsel systems
c. criminal justice systems
d. indigent assistance systems

6. This court officer keeps the court records and provides a pool of jurors for cases that go to trial.
a. general assistant
b. bailiff
c. court reporter
d. clerk of the court

7. The chief legal officer for a state is the
a. state solicitor general.
b. state magistrate judge.
c. state attorney general.
d. state prosecutor.

8. A defendant who is released based on his or her promise to return to court has received this.
a. a reprieve
b. release-on-recognizance
c. luck
d. cash bond

9. What is the term for the expectation that the courtroom workgroup settles similar cases in a similar manner?
a. disposition
b. *voir dire*
c. going rate
d. grabbable area

10. This participant in the criminal justice system helps those who cannot afford bail to get out of jail while awaiting trial.
a. bail agent
b. defense attorney
c. bailiff
d. bail enforcement agent

True/False

1. There is no limit to the prosecutor's powers. _____

2. The prosecutor's office never represents the state's interests in other areas of the legal community. _____

3. Judges act as a check-and-balance to the discretion of prosecutors. _____

4. Nearly half of the states elect judges. _____

5. The president appoints the U.S. attorney general. _____

6. Courts are required by law to provide victim/witness services and programs. _____

7. The Justice Department is responsible for many activities that are not connected to the prosecution of cases. _____

8. The defense attorney acts as a gatekeeper in deciding which cases enter the criminal justice system. _____

9. The defense attorney ensures that the prosecution adequately proves the charges. _____

10. Members of the courtroom workgroup usually do not cooperate. _____

Fill in the Blank

1. _____ write pre-sentence investigation reports recommending sentences to the judge.

2. In _____, the Supreme Court determined that evidence may be admitted if the fault for a bad warrant rests with the court and not with the police.

3. _____ counsel is when a judge has practicing members of the bar represent indigent defendants.

4. Legal variables such as seriousness of the offense and the defendant's prior record are factored into the _____.

5. The _____ maintains order in the courtroom.

6. A _____ signs search warrants.

7. _____ ensure that the best interests of children are considered in juvenile court.

8. _____ is when the U.S. president nominates a judge.

9. Drafting legal documents is one of the five categories of activities that _____ engage in.

10. The prosecution of all federal criminal statutes is coordinated by the Department of Justice _____.

Find a Flash
Read the two news flashes in Chapter 9 carefully, noting how they illustrate issues covered in the chapter.

- *Whose Side Are You On?* and *It's a Tough Job, but Someone Has to Do It* review prosecutorial responsibilities, burdens, and conflicts of interest.

Use the library or search the web to find two news items that exemplify, explain, or even appear to contradict topics from Chapter 9. Write short summaries of these news items in the spaces provided. If possible, find one local story and one national story. Give your news flashes short titles that explain what they are about. Suggested news flash topics are listed below.

Prosecutors
Federal-level prosecution
State-level prosecution
Defense attorneys
Public defenders
Judges
Judicial selection
Defendants, victims, or witnesses
Pretrial release decisions

News Flash #1

Title

News Flash #2

Title

What Agency Am I?

Peruse the following descriptions taken from the websites of federal criminal justice-related agencies, programs, and bureaus. Find the organization that matches it in the list and write it in the blank space provided. Hint: Use the web addresses in the list to check the organizations' websites.

A. I handle the application of all federal criminal laws except those specifically assigned to other divisions. I oversee criminal matters as well as certain civil litigation. In addition to my direct litigation responsibilities, I formulate and implement criminal enforcement policy and provide advice and assistance. I approve or monitor sensitive areas of law enforcement such as participation in the Witness Security Program and the use of electronic surveillance; advise the attorney general, Congress, the Office of Management Budget, and the White House on matters of criminal law; provide legal advice and assistance to federal prosecutors and investigative agencies; and provide leadership for coordinating international as well as federal, state, and local law enforcement matters.

Who Am I? _____

B. I was authorized in 1816, and my jurisdiction ranges from criminal justice to antitrust and intellectual property law. One of my duties is to conduct confirmation hearings for judicial nominees to the Supreme Court, court of appeals, and district court.

Who Am I? _____

C. I supervise and conduct government litigation in the United States Supreme Court. My chief officer determines the cases in which the government will seek Supreme Court review and the positions the government will take before the court. My staff attorneys help to prepare the petitions, briefs, and other papers filed by the government in Supreme Court litigation. I review all cases decided adversely to the government in the lower courts to determine whether they should be appealed and, if so, what position should be taken. My chief officer also determines whether the government will participate as an *amicus curiae* or intervene in cases in any appellate court.

Who Am I? _____

List

Department of Justice Criminal Division	http://www.usdoj.gov/criminal/criminal-home.html
Federal Judiciary	http://www.uscourts.gov
National Institute of Justice	http://www.ojp.usdoj.gov/nij
Office of the Attorney General	http://www.usdoj.gov/ag
Office of the Solicitor General	http://www.usdoj.gov/osg
U.S. Senate Committee on the Judiciary	http://judiciary.senate.gov
U.S. Supreme Court	http://www.supremecourtus.gov

Word Search

Instructions: Fill in the blanks of the definitions below with the correct word, then find the word in the puzzle!

```
M M F Y B L C D R D I V J E Q E B R U J O T Y B K U H U R L
B I I R S X F J L X U Z B X S S O W V O C T F F E C R B X T
X S P F W T X I N N P V K L T M S A R D X A U Y G W C I Y G
J S Y S A G G O U O P K Y Q J S M D Z C I S U C U I G T U Z
Q O M Y Z N N K P H I R M G S W N M Y C T D Y V X R R Z A J
T U A H I V D F Q Z Z T C E W Z Y Q J O Z D X T B G F W V X
N R S C Q R Y J M G B I F T Q N P U U X U E E G J C Q I Q
S I V R O X T C P C A C E S Z P Z L C R Z O E Y N B D X J I
X B H Q P U W P S P H T N V O P C I X T R U D O J G G R Q U
D A M F Q H R C N E T J A H Z P D W P A J V C H A C Q R N R
F R Y V U V H T B W Z V U P E R S D Q D V V O S F T P W L K
J P Z V D S H G R F S O U I M Y N I S M Q H O Q H W G Z K L
Z L M X F A N O Z E J V K B G F D A D I X E Z G H X M H Z O
H A M F X O P E N E P L E A W F D E Q N S L D R N M W A K R
Z N X H A X E G Y H S O Z G V U E P Z I I P L P G R C W J Y
D S N X R A M Y U C D R R S Y O E H A S P Y E V T S F Q K A
U W G Q D H Q X E Z T A I T R R S B D T Q R J P G B O T R H
Z C N Z G U U G H W M K E B E C I S X R M X A Z C P T Q E L
E J K B Z W M U G A E H U I H R K V R A N K N A B E P R L A
M C P P A B Y U T D A S L I X M D Z T T H A F D W Q N C C E
B L L U P C F Y D Y Y Q L U J R S N W O M B C I D X P X F G
Z G I S O W R Z D U A D X D Q W L A T R H G E J N G X T H L
G O I N G R A T E Z A N S Q G I T Z E F T U O H Q K O K I P
A X A P W Z D M G D O C X V O A T Q G H R E E K F Q S B U O
J O F O P G Z U V Q B A I L A G E N T D Q N J J Y N T A Q W
V B A I P J S O N Y T C V B K L Y Q T T H P L E M H N D T R
Y Y T M I C C K T U G X X S P H P G A R A Q U R P Z R P X A
V X L Z E A V I D R J T S G H B Z V G L F O J I U J I W P I
Q Q M T T E U C H D C H Q G J A U H Z B A I H Q K C A Z T
B J G E I Z R A F R O V Z X S P Z W T A A B V I V F L U A A
```

Definitions

1. A _____ works for a private, for-profit company that provides money for suspects to be released from jail.

2. A _____ is appointed by the court to protect the interests of the child.

3. The _____ of the court is the primary administrative officer of a court who manages non-judicial functions.

4. The _____ is responsible for mechanical necessities of the court, including scheduling courtrooms, managing case flow, administering personnel, procuring furniture, and preparing budgets.

5. The _____ records and transcribes an official verbatim record of the legal proceedings of the court.

6. The final determination of a case or other matter by a court or other judicial entity is the _____.

7. _____ describes how similar cases have been settled by a given set of judges, prosecutors, and attorneys.

8. The _____ is also called "merit selection."

Chapter 10
The Disposition: Plea Bargaining, Trial, and Sentencing

Learning Objectives
After reading this chapter, students should be able to:

1. Understand the nature of the disposition.
2. Explain plea bargaining and why it is important.
3. Understand the arguments for the abolishment of plea bargaining.
4. Discuss why a trial is a relatively rare event.
5. Explain the purpose of pretrial motions.
6. Describe the motives of the prosecutor and the defense attorney in opening arguments.
7. Understand the importance of the jury system versus government power.
8. Describe the role of the jurors.
9. Explain evidence and how it is handled.
10. Describe the stresses on victims and witnesses.
11. Explain victims' rights.
12. Describe the factors that guide sentencing.

Chapter Summary and Key Concepts
Chapter 10 describes how the courts dispose of cases, including plea bargaining and jury trials.

Plea Bargaining
- Plea bargaining is often criticized because it appears as if the offender escapes the full impact of justice.
- A plea bargain does not determine guilt or innocence.
- In a plea bargain, defendants plead guilty or *nolo contendere* in exchange for a lighter sentence.
- Types of plea bargains include vertical pleas, horizontal pleas, reduced-sentence pleas, and avoidance-of-stigma pleas.
- Most cases are settled in the plea bargaining process, and only a few cases go to a jury trial.

The Trial
- Criminal trials are relatively rare.
- The rights of defendants in criminal trials are derived from the Bill of Rights.
- Prior to opening statements, each side may file pretrial motions to gain the most favorable circumstances and to limit the evidence from the other side.
- Frequent pretrial motions include: motion for dismissal of charges, motion for continuance, motion for discovery, motion for severance of defendants, motion for severance of offenses, motion for the suppression of evidence, motion to determine competency, and motion for change of venue.
- No evidence is presented during opening arguments.

- The prosecution makes the first opening argument, telling why it believes that the defendant is guilty. The prosecution will outline the case and tell the jury of the types of evidence to be presented.
- The defense attorney counters the prosecution's version of the case.
- The prosecution introduces evidence and witnesses.
- During this presentation, the defense may object to questions asked by the prosecutor or answers given by a witness.
- The defense may then cross-examine the witnesses.
- The prosecutor may question the witness again, followed by questions from the defense.
- After the prosecution presents its evidence and witnesses, the defense may present its own evidence and witnesses.
- The prosecution may cross-examine these witnesses, followed by redirect questions from the defense and re-cross-examination by the prosecution.
- Closing arguments follow, and the case goes to the jury.
- The formation of a jury requires several steps: creation of the mastery jury list, formation of the *venire*, and *voir dire*.
- Jury selection is subject to influence by the prosecution and defense through *voir dire*. A potential juror may be excluded by challenge for cause or peremptory challenge.
- A conviction or acquittal requires a unanimous vote.
- Defendants who are found guilty are sentenced by the judge, who has considerable discretion in deciding the sentence.
- Cases that usually do not get a jury trial are those in which the penalty is not serious, cases with a juvenile defendant, or cases when the defense requests a bench trial.
- In a bench trial, a judge decides on guilt or innocence and passes sentence.

Sentencing
- The two primary types of sentencing philosophies are indeterminate sentencing and determinate sentencing.
- The indeterminate sentence is fashioned to fit the offender; the determinate sentence is fashioned to fit the crime.
- Mandatory minimum sentences, a form of determinate sentencing, do not allow probation and specify incarceration for a term not less than a specified number of years.
- To increase the voice and input of the victim, many states have adopted victim-rights legislation.

Key Terms

bench trial
A trial that takes place before a judge, but without a jury, in which the judge makes the decision. Sometimes called a *court trial*.

beyond a reasonable doubt
Refers to the highest level of proof required to win a case. This level of proof is necessary in criminal cases in order to procure a guilty verdict.

determinate sentence
A prison term that is determined by law and states a specific period of time to be served. Sentencing grids or guidelines are usually employed in calculating the sentence. For example, an armed robbery conviction might call for a 30-year sentence in jail, regardless of the circumstances of the offender or the crime.

directed verdict of acquittal
An order from a trial judge to the jury stating that the jury must acquit the accused because the prosecution has not proved its case. A judge may not "direct a verdict of guilty," however, as such an order would violate the accused's right to a jury trial.

indeterminate sentence
A prison term that does not state a specific period of time to be served or date of release. Such a sentence will specify a range of time to be served, such as 10 to 20 years.

hung jury
A term describing a jury in a criminal case that is deadlocked or that cannot produce a unanimous verdict.

impeach
The discrediting of a witness. This may be done by proving that the witness has lied or has been inconsistent, or by producing contrary evidence.

mandatory minimum sentence
A sentence determined by law that establishes the minimum length of prison time that may be served for a crime.

plea bargain
A compromise between the defendant, the defendant's attorney, and the prosecutor in which the defendant agrees to plead guilty or no contest in return for reduction of the charges' severity, dismissal of some charges, further information about the crime or about others involved in it, or the prosecutor's agreement to recommend a desired sentence. Plea bargains require a judge's approval.

presumptive sentence
A sentence that may be adjusted by the judge depending on aggravating or mitigating factors.

redirect examination
The questioning of a witness about issues uncovered during cross-examination.

venire
The list or pool from which jurors are chosen.

voir dire
French for "to see, to speak." Refers to the questioning of jurors by a judge and/or attorneys to determine if individual jurors are appropriate for a particular jury panel. Jurors may be dismissed by the judge or attorneys.

Short Answer Questions

Plea bargaining has been called a necessary evil. Why is it necessary? Why is it evil?

_____
_____
_____
_____
_____
_____
_____
_____
_____

What are the various stages of the criminal court trial? Which are the most time-consuming and which appear to be simply legal hurdles?

_____
_____
_____
_____
_____
_____
_____

What rights does a criminal defendant have in the trial? Are these rights excessive or are they reasonable to ensure fairness?

What is the difference between an indeterminate sentence and a determinate sentence? How does each of these treat the issue of discretion? Can discretion ever be eliminated from the criminal justice system? Should it be eliminated?

What is the mandatory minimum sentence? Are you as a taxpayer willing to pay for a type of sentencing that takes money from schools and other public projects and gives it to the criminal justice system to build more prisons?

Study Guide Questions

Multiple Choice

1. The first step in a criminal trial is the
   a. indictment.
   b. plea.
   c. true-bill.
   d. disposition.

2. A trial in which a judge decides on guilt or innocence and passes sentence is called a
   a. criminal trial.
   b. jury trial.
   c. judge trial.
   d. bench trial.

3. By pleading guilty or *nolo contendere* to a lesser included charge, the defendant can reduce a potentially harsh sentence. What kind of plea is this?
   a. avoidance-of-stigma plea
   b. horizontal plea
   c. vertical plea
   d. reduced-sentence plea

4. An attorney can attempt to exclude a juror by
a. challenge to the array.
b. peremptory challenge.
c. motion for a new trial.
d. motion for dismissal.

5. The defense may file this in order to obtain documents and a list of witnesses that the prosecution plans to call.
a. motion for a mistrial
b. motion for change of venue
c. motion for continuance
d. motion for discovery

6. The jury pool is called the
a. *venire.*
b. *voir dire.*
c. *vox populi.*
d. *lex talionis.*

7. A defendant can use this to plead guilty to a charge in exchange for other charges being dropped.
a. reduced-sentence plea
b. vertical plea
c. horizontal plea
d. avoidance-of-stigma plea

8. A jury in which some of the members vote for guilt and some vote for innocence is called a
a. *voir dire.*
b. tampered jury.
c. hung jury.
d. wasted jury.

9. This is when the defense asks the judge to rule that the prosecution has not presented a compelling case against the defendant.
a. impeachment
b. directed verdict of acquittal
c. redirect examination
d. bench trial

10. This is the questioning of prospective jurors to determine if they have the necessary qualifications to serve.
a. *venire*
b. redirect examination
c. motion to question
d. *voir dire*

True/False

1. Plea bargaining does not focus on determining guilt or innocence. _____

2. The rights of criminal defendants are derived mostly from ancient sources. _____

3. The prosecution is first to make an opening argument. _____

4. Ideally, determinate sentencing assigns a fixed sentence to each offender convicted of a particular crime. _____

5. Mandatory minimum laws are very amenable to probation and alternative sentencing. _____

6. Plea bargaining benefits no one. _____

7. Trials can last months for complicated cases. _____

8. Motions are important in a trial. _____

9. Many states allow a jury of six for some types of cases. _____

10. Criminal trials happen relatively often. _____

Fill in the Blank

1. By pleading _____, the defendant waives the right to a jury trial and is sentenced as if there were a determination of guilt.

2. The _____ may be compiled from voter registration records, driver's license lists, and utility customer lists.

3. Several provisions in the _____ speak directly to defendants' rights in criminal trials.

4. Both real evidence and testimony may be called _____ evidence.

5. A(n) _____ is when a defendant is able to claim that he or she was elsewhere during the commission of a crime.

6. The defense attorney may _____ the witness after the prosecution's questioning.

7. In _____, the Supreme Court established that the use of peremptory challenges to racially manipulate a jury violates the defendant's right to an impartial jury.

8. The decision in _____ affirmed the constitutionality of the denial of bail and pretrial release for a suspect who may be dangerous.

9. A motion for _____ requests that a defendant charged with several crimes be tried separately on all or some of the charges.

10. The _____ allows judges limited discretion to depart from the guidelines.

Find a Flash
Read the two news flashes in Chapter 10 carefully, noting how they illustrate issues covered in the chapter.

- *Their Day in Court* reviews a typical day in a circuit court.
- *Seeing Things* examines the unreliability of eyewitness testimony.

Use the library or search the web to find two news items that exemplify, explain, or even appear to contradict topics from Chapter 10. Write short summaries of these news items in the spaces provided. If possible, find one local story and one national story. Give your news flashes short titles that explain what they are about. Suggested news flash topics are listed below.

Plea bargaining
Elements of the trial
Evidence
Victims' rights
Sentencing
Indeterminate sentences
Determinate sentences
Mandatory minimum sentences

News Flash #1

Title _____

News Flash #2

Title

What Agency Am I?

Peruse the following descriptions taken from the websites of federal criminal justice-related agencies, programs, and bureaus. Find the organization that matches it in the list and write it in the blank space provided. Hint: Use the web addresses in the list to check the organizations' websites.

A. I coordinate the use of alternative dispute resolution (ADR) for the Department of Justice. I am responsible for ADR policy matters and training, assisting lawyers in selecting the right cases for dispute resolution, and finding appropriate neutrals to serve as mediators, arbitrators, and neutral evaluators. I also coordinate the Interagency ADR Working Group, an organization that promotes the use of ADR throughout federal executive branch agencies.

Who Am I? _____

B. In consultation with the attorney general, I assist the president in the exercise of executive clemency as authorized under Article II, Section 2, of the Constitution. All requests for executive clemency for federal offenses are directed to me for investigation and review. I prepare the department's recommendation to the president for final disposition of each application. Executive clemency may take several forms, including pardon, commutation of sentence, remission of fine or restitution, and reprieve.

Who Am I? _____

C. I am the education and research agency for the federal courts. Congress created me in 1967 to promote improvements in judicial administration in the U.S. courts.

Who Am I? _____

List

Department of Justice Criminal Division	http://www.usdoj.gov/criminal/criminal-home.html
Federal Judicial Center	http://www.fjc.gov
National Institute of Corrections	http://nicic.org/
National Institute of Justice	http://www.ojp.usdoj.gov/nij
Office of Dispute Resolution	http://www.usdoj.gov/odr
Office of the Attorney General	http://www.usdoj.gov/ag
Office of the Pardon Attorney	http://www.usdoj.gov/pardon

Word Search

Instructions: Fill in the blanks of the definitions below with the correct word, then find the word in the puzzle!

```
Z S W X O H R E A S O N A B L E D O U B T J B J V Y Y G E P
Z T A H B E W X R E D I R E C T E X A M I N A T I O N M F O
S S D G C N C M Y F O A L M Y U X Z E S K Y S Y I C I K F I
H B M R J X M N G V D L T J H G Z T W D J F P C M R V R M U
T J G Q B Y Q K E H O E W G T T K L O D G S M K P K K A A M
Z C G K L A L S Y T O C Z T W Q B O K G X H H W B I T T D F
N W D G E Y T O X R N N C K F C K L W Q W P C L E M G E F J
D W O G R C F R R H C E E F A A W W I Q M P L R W P S J I G
Z P M V I V M B G G L T S S A K Z X D T W A W J F E W O H W
J F D D N I A P R Q H N V E C Z J T X X I Q S I U A Y O V C
S P F J E S N V Q B P E U D T U F A N R Y K N A B C R Z Q C
X I U D V O D H T O N S Q Z O A R A T R U N P I Q H E U N A
O L U D V I A J K I I E S E S Y N H X C H U N G J U R Y F Y
E P Z K H C T S X D A T F W M U C I J Y K Y V S L R L O A M
K V R O O X O Z T U G A S R R N K E M U R W H Q C E L E M B
L T K X B P R I R R R N A U E V Q U B R L T C D I N Z H A A
F M M V I N Y S A T A I K B O D P H L Y E S C B V C C H E F
T V Y Z K D M R H G B M W U K N T G V L K T F C R G B I V U
Z J T Z V A I I V M A R B A Q H F U D L I I E J Q T E T I F
Y B W R C U N A P X E E U G A L R M S K R G Q D A F B P M D
L B Z K N X I B R K L T X Q Q X A O I U O Q E R I D R I O V
J T P P F Z M F X M P E N V J G M G B W Y V S P X N H V V N
I Q I S C O U D V N N D N S S C L G A O C S J P C Q Q H Z D
X W N H M F M R G I J N W V S U Y M J F B C M X A S Q D J D
P I U T N R R K D S U I J N C J N I Q Y Y N L T I F B M X Q
R B V G A M B J S Y K Q H Y J W K Q A K D A V T O K J D W V
P E C N E T N E S E V I T P M U S E R P J B R T Z O V L L C
J P N U J F L Q J S D Z R Q R W F R H K Z K A L M E N X T O
B U I U X R A W E R I X A M M C T T O Q F W B T S P L W L C
I X L B T V K M P Q D I R E C T E D V E R D I C T J V U T S
```

Definitions

1. A _____ takes place without a jury, before a judge who makes the decision.

2. The _____ is determined by law and states a specific period of time to be served.

3. A _____ is one that is deadlocked or that cannot produce a unanimous verdict.

4. To _____ is to discredit a witness.

5. An _____ does not state a specific period of time to be served or date of release.

6. The _____ sentence establishes the minimum length of prison time that may be served for a crime.

7. A _____ is a compromise between the defendant, the defendant's attorney, and the prosecutor in which the defendant agrees to plead guilty or no contest in return for sentencing considerations.

8. A _____ may be adjusted by the judge depending on aggravating or mitigating factors.

9. _____ is the questioning of a witness about issues uncovered during cross-examination.

10. _____ is the list or pool from which jurors are chosen.

11. The questioning of jurors by a judge and/or attorneys to determine if individual jurors are appropriate for a particular jury panel is called _____.

12. Beyond a _____ refers to the highest level of proof required to win a case.

13. A _____ of acquittal is an order from a trial judge to the jury stating that the jury must acquit the accused because the prosecution has not proved its case.

Match the Case

Part Three
The Role of the Courts

Draw a line from the case to its outcome.

Duncan v. Louisiana	The Supreme Court effectively reinstated the death penalty, finding that it did not constitute cruel and unusual punishment as long as its implementation was fair.
Argersinger v. Hamlin	This is the first case in which the U.S. Supreme Court applied the constitutional right to counsel to a specific prosecution.
United States v. Salerno	The Supreme Court established that the use of peremptory challenges to racially manipulate a jury violates the defendant's right to an impartial jury.
Batson v. Kentucky	Under the Sixth Amendment, defendants charged with serious crimes are entitled to a jury trial.
Furman v. Georgia	The decision set forth that the administration of the death penalty constituted cruel and unusual punishment, not the death penalty itself.
Powell v. State of Alabama	Denying bail and pretrial release to a suspect who may be a danger to society is constitutional.
United States v. Leon	The accused has the right to an attorney whether the crime is a misdemeanor or a felony.
Gregg v. Georgia	Evidence may be admitted if the fault for a bad warrant rests with the court and not with the police.

Chapter 11
History of Control

Learning Objectives
After reading this chapter, you should be able to:

1. Describe why societies use control.
2. Compare and contrast ancient and modern methods of social control.
3. Discuss the early use of corporal punishment and the various methods used.
4. Discuss the early use of economic punishment and the various methods used.
5. Describe the means of control in colonial America.
6. Discuss the eras in the development of the penitentiary.
7. Compare and contrast the Pennsylvania and Auburn prison systems.
8. Describe the contributions of Alexander Maconochie, Sir Walter Crofton, and Zebulon Brockway.
9. Describe the history of capital punishment.
10. Discuss the common arguments for and against capital punishment.

Chapter Summary and Key Concepts
Chapter 11 explores the history, purpose, and means of the control of offenders.

The History of Control
- Human societies require their members to follow rules. Members who do not follow the rules must be controlled for the sake of the society.
- Violations of the rules bring mild rebukes to extreme violence as groups seek to make members conform.
- Ancient societies did not have organized systems to deal with offenders. In many societies, justice tended to be a private matter.
- Corporal punishment, inflicting physical harm on the body, was a primary means to control and extract revenge from offenders.
- The major formalized means of inflicting pain were torture, flogging, branding, mutilation, humiliation, and shock death.
- Dispositions that required labor rather than pain included forcing offenders to work on galley ships and in workhouses, and exiling them to foreign lands.

Prisons: Development, Reforms, and Penal Philosophies
- Early American institutions were locally controlled and imprisoned different types of offenders together.
- Two reform-type prison systems emerged during the first half of the 19th century: the Pennsylvania System and the Auburn System, both emphasizing silence and penitence.
- European countries developed the Irish System, which was designed not just to punish, but also to increase the inmate's success in returning to free society. The three most well-known examples were developed by Alexander Maconochie, Sir Walter Crofton, and Zebulon Brockway.

- Alexander Maconochie popularized the indeterminate sentence.
- Sir Walter Crofton instituted the early-release ticket-of-leave system.
- At New York's Elmira Reformatory, Zebulon Brockway used an early type of parole officer to keep track of released inmates.
- In the early 20th century, work was considered useful for keeping inmates occupied, rehabilitating inmates, and offsetting the cost of incarceration.
- U.S. prisons acknowledged rehabilitation as a primary goal around 1930.
- Reasons for rehabilitation were new developments in how science treated illness and the 1931 Wickersham Commission report.
- In the 1960s, inmates became politically active in demanding changes in their surroundings, and the courts began to specify inmates' rights.
- The retributive era began around 1970 and continues to the present. This era features replacing indeterminate sentencing with determinate sentencing, making treatment voluntary, and the abolition of parole.

Capital Punishment
- The most extreme and controversial form of control is capital punishment.
- Historically, punishment by death was common, and a number of ways were devised to kill offenders.
- In the 20th century, death sentences began to be carried out with few witnesses and in the most painless way believed possible.
- Arguments for capital punishment include general and specific deterrence and retribution.
- Arguments against capital punishment include religious and spiritual concerns about killing; belief that it does not deter; race, gender, and class issues about who is selected for death; and fear of executing the innocent.

Key Terms

congregate-and-silent system
A style of control pioneered by the Auburn System in which inmates were allowed to eat and work together during the day, but forbidden to speak, and locked alone in their cells at night.

general deterrence
A method of control in which the punishment of a single offender sets an example for the rest of society.

just deserts
A philosophy that states that an offender who commits a heinous crime deserves death.

marks-of-commendation system
An incarceration philosophy developed by Alexander Maconochie in which inmates earned the right to be released, as well as privileges, goods, and services.

retribution model
A style of control in which offenders are punished as severely as possible for a crime and in which rehabilitation is not attempted.

separate-and-silent system
A method of penal control pioneered by Philadelphia's Eastern State Penitentiary in which inmates were kept from seeing or talking to one another. This method is comparable to solitary confinement in modern prisons.

specific deterrence
A method of control in which an offender is prevented from committing more crimes by either imprisonment or death.

Short Answer Questions

How were people punished before there were prisons? Are modern prisons an improvement over ancient punishments? If you were convicted of a serious crime, what method of punishment, either ancient or modern, would you choose?

_____
_____
_____
_____
_____
_____
_____
_____
_____
_____
_____
_____

Compare and contrast the Pennsylvania prison model with the Auburn prison model. Which of these models most restricted the inmates? In which prison would you choose to serve your prison sentence?

_____
_____
_____
_____
_____
_____
_____
_____
_____
_____

Discuss the arguments for and against capital punishment. Why is the United States one of the few democracies still using the death penalty? What is your position on this controversial topic?

_____
_____
_____
_____
_____
_____
_____
_____
_____
_____

What are the theoretical reasons used to justify capital punishment? How have these reasons fared when subjected to scientific research?

Explain how the medical model was used to justify rehabilitation. Is rehabilitation worth pursuing in modern corrections? Can we afford not to?

Study Guide Questions

Multiple Choice

1. This penal system allowed inmates to eat and work together but prohibited speaking and face-to-face contact.
   a. separate-and-silent system
   b. Irish system
   c. congregate-and-silent system
   d. Auburn system

2. The era of retribution changed incarceration in these ways.
   a. probation; parole; rehabilitative therapy
   b. determinate sentencing; voluntary treatment; abolition of parole
   c. determinate sentencing; probation; voluntary treatment
   d. voluntary treatment; indeterminate sentencing; abolition of parole

3. Inmates could earn release, as well as privileges, goods, and services with this system.
   a. marks-of-commendation system
   b. separate-and-silent system
   c. parole system
   d. early-release system

4. The Supreme Court halted execution of the insane with this case.
   a. *Ford v. Wainwright*
   b. *Argersinger v. Hamlin*
   c. *Furman v. Georgia*
   d. *Terry v. Ohio*

5. This form of punishment sent inmates from their home countries and provided new lands and colonies with labor.
   a. forced labor
   b. incarceration
   c. transportation
   d. torture

6. This punishment sentenced an offender to death and reprieved him or her at the last moment before execution.
   a. torture
   b. shock death
   c. false execution
   d. burning-in-effigy

7. In 1792, this jail was converted into the first U.S. penitentiary.
   a. Reading Gaol
   b. Cherry Hill Jail
   c. Alcatraz
   d. Walnut Street Jail

8. This Supreme Court decision established limits for the execution of the mentally retarded.
   a. *Weeks v. United States*
   b. *Furman v. Georgia*
   c. *Ford v. Wainwright*
   d. *Atkins v. Virginia*

9. This system isolated inmates so that they would not contaminate one another with anti-social thoughts.
   a. separate-and-silent system
   b. congregate-and-silent system
   c. ticket-of-leave system
   d. silent-and-silent system

10. Sir Walter Crofton invented this system in which inmates received conditional release and were supervised by local police.
    a. Auburn system
    b. ticket-of-leave system
    c. Irish system
    d. congregate-and-silent system

True/False

1. The penitentiary originated in the United States. _____

2. Alexander Maconochie believed that brutality and cruelty debased societies that used such methods for social control. _____

3. Zebulon Brockway was often known as "Paddler Brockway." _____

4. The philosophy that work is healthy for both the inmate and society is relatively recent. _____

5. Courts maintain a "hands off" policy regarding prisons. _____

6. The idea of incarceration as the only punishment for convicted offenders is relatively recent. _____

7. During the retributive era, the primary function of parole moved from treatment to supervision. _____

8. The Pennsylvania and Auburn systems emphasized vigorous social interaction. _____

9. Death has been a common form of punishment throughout history. _____

10. Penal reform progressed smoothly from brutality to humane treatment. _____

Fill in the Blank

1. _____ originated the marks-of-commendation system.

2. _____ ran the Elmira Reformatory, which used volunteers to keep up with released inmates.

3. The case _____ helped set guidelines for what constitutes cruel and unusual punishment in prison and the circumstances under which prison officials are liable.

4. _____ Prison became known for its use of the congregate-and-silent system.

5. _____ began the ticket-of-leave system.

6. Abolition of parole is a change instituted in the _____ era.

7. The idea of _____ stresses that executed individuals will never commit another crime.

8. The Quakers preferred _____ to flogging.

9. Some critics say capital punishment is a violation of the "cruel and unusual punishments" clause of the _____ Amendment.

10. The _____ Penitentiary was characterized by the separate-and-silent system.

Find a Flash

Read the two news flashes in Chapter 11 carefully, noting how they illustrate issues covered in the chapter.

- *Spare the Rod, Spoil the Child, Save the Inmate* looks at the selective use of corporal punishment.
- *Federal Prison Industries* reviews modern prison labor practices.

Use the library or search the web to find two news items that exemplify, explain, or even appear to contradict topics from Chapter 11. Write short summaries of these news items in the spaces provided. If possible, find one local story and one national story. Give your news flashes short titles that explain what they are about. Suggested news flash topics are listed below.

Economic punishment
Modern U.S. Prisons
Historical U.S. Prisons
Penal reform
Inmate rehabilitation
Retributive penal practices
Capital punishment

News Flash #1

Title

News Flash #2

Title

What Agency Am I?

Peruse the following descriptions taken from the websites of federal criminal justice-related agencies, programs, and bureaus. Find the organization that matches it in the list and write it in the blank space provided. Hint: Use the web addresses in the list to check the organizations' websites.

A. I am an independent judicial agency that establishes sentencing policies and practices for the federal courts, including guidelines prescribing the appropriate form and severity of punishment for offenders convicted of federal crimes. I also advise and assist Congress and the executive branch in developing effective and efficient crime policy and collecting, analyzing, researching, and distributing information on federal crime and sentencing issues.

Who Am I? _____

B. Part of the Commerce Department, I advance national security, foreign policy, and economic interests. I regulate the export of sensitive goods and technologies; enforce export control, anti-boycott, and public safety laws; assist other countries on export control and strategic trade issues; assist U.S. industry in complying with international arms control agreements; and monitor the viability of the U.S. defense industrial base, ensuring that it is capable of satisfying U.S. national and homeland security needs.

Who Am I? _____

C. I am a Department of the Interior police agency that protects public safety and resources across 264 million acres of public land. I protect cultural and historical sites from vandalism; eradicate drug-manufacturing laboratories and marijuana fields; ensure the humane treatment of wild horses and burros; guard against the dumping of hazardous wastes and other pollutants; and prevent the theft and damage of timber, rare cactus plants, minerals, and other valuable publicly owned resources.

Who Am I? _____

List

Bureau of Land Management Law Enforcement	http://www.blm.gov/nhp/pubs/brochures/law
Federal Judicial Center	http://www.fjc.gov
Office of Dispute Resolution	http://www.usdoj.gov/odr
Office of the Attorney General	http://www.usdoj.gov/ag
Office of the Pardon Attorney	http://www.usdoj.gov/pardon
U.S. Bureau of Industry and Security	http://www.bxa.doc.gov
U.S. Sentencing Commission	http://www.ussc.gov

Word Search

Instructions: Fill in the blanks of the definitions below with the correct word, then find the word in the puzzle!

```
D O Q H G Q E J V E Z J Y X C T N F T S B M P U R T M D Q I
L S R N Y I P K K W R D J H S G C A O Q F E M B Z B M I P G
Z B Y W X F X O M L F L V G H S J K P T Q P B G S R A F N E
S J E W L W L Q N P B K L S I O E O P U F S F T C V Y K L Y
P K U F F Z X F M L Z M M V C I U W K G O V S R V Q D Z U O
Z N E S A N R T N H E D A I T I F G T X S R O J G Q I Y F F
U B X Z T F Z X Q K K Q R L S K A L M T F N U Y L E I M Y V
W J C G U D G Q K U S G K E P Z F X C N E X N F E C Z G C U
P J T G J X E C B V L D S D E S A I J E T K W F O N P N Z J
W J O S Z H A S H H C V O E C J T C P L N J I A Z E H C U U
S I V I I M P N E A I G F F I O Q U Y I S E N A Z R Z H G Q
E B F D C T F T V R D T C W F Q Y T G S Q A N G T R I H O E
C F J J M B J R M A T U O Z I B H V C D K E Y M F E S A J H
H L S D T O T Z P H S S M H C E A L V N Q G S Q A T R N A S
B R U N U Z O J Z J Y Y M U D E W C M A T K U P Q E Q O K W
E J E A A C M N V V I E E U E C O D Q E Q K Z D A D R B G J
O E D T C S X C L I F D N I T Z M K T T K N K D Q L Y N M H
C P O I R D Y H U B R T D H E Z K V G A U A N M A A Q F P M
A P R N O I N O L Y E L A B R R O B M G B W T J L R Y C S F
K K Y D M B B S R R O T T W R X G L J E P U R V D E A Y C E
U V V E O T I U D J K P I Y E M J S I R Y Q U Z B N H P D C
Z K L F J Y P H T F U I O W N R U L P G L N B U H E W N S P
I Y B X C R X R H I R X N E C J R S M N K R M H Z G M P H L
R P R E W Y B V B Y O A K L E Q Y V D O L A D U Q R C E Y L
Z T H S M U N I R T O N Z T I H L M Y C M V J Q C I F Z S L
G E X A M L G M Q Y N M R T I Q E W O Q I H W P D H Q W G
R O X N B W V X G P W K H O U I W B G L U P B G E D S I D J
S V R B I X X O U I V E J A D E R S R D N Y B Q T K C Z B C
U K D L A A B I R R C P P T N E L I S D N A E T A R A P E S
N D B D C X D S G D A J W M K F L F A T Y G C X Q E E Z U D
```

Definitions

1. In the _____ system inmates were allowed to eat and work together during the day, but forbidden to speak.

2. According to the _____ theory, the punishment of a single offender sets an example for the rest of society.

3. According to the _____ theory, an offender who commits a heinous crime deserves death.

4. _____ was an incarceration philosophy in which inmates earned the right to be released, as well as privileges, goods, and services.

5. Using the _____, offenders are punished as severely as possible for a crime and rehabilitation is not attempted.

6. In the _____ system, inmates were kept from seeing or talking to one another.

7. According to the theory of _____, an offender is prevented from committing more crimes by either imprisonment or death.

160

Chapter 12
The Contemporary Prison

Learning Objectives
After reading this chapter, you should be able to:

1. Understand how prisons are an example of a "total institution."
2. Appreciate the ways in which the inmate subculture develops.
3. Discuss argot roles.
4. Compare and contrast the Attica and New Mexico prison riots.
5. Describe how civilian work roles in the prison differ from those in society.
6. List some special job functions of correctional officers.
7. Identify some aspects or themes of the correctional officers' work.
8. Discuss the "hands-off" doctrine.
9. Describe special problems or points of contention between inmate rights and institutional requirements.
10. Compare and contrast private prisons with government-run prisons.

Chapter Summary and Key Concepts
Chapter 12 examines the institution of the prison and how it affects inmates and prison staff.

Work and Life in the Prison
- The prison is a closed institution where everything is tightly controlled and structured.
- Inmates develop terms, called an *argot*, for the various roles they take in order to adapt to imprisonment.
- Prison gangs have replaced many of the traditional, individual argot roles.
- Pelican Bay State Prison is an example of a maximum-security prison that recalls the separate-and-silent systems of early U.S. prisons.
- The two most infamous prison riots are the 1971 Attica Prison riot and the 1980 New Mexico State Prison riot.
- Guards, medical technicians, treatment specialists, administrators, secretaries, and clergy are examples of the types of staff who work in the prison.
- The most prevalent staff position is that of the correctional officer.

Courts and the Prison
- Prior to the 1960s, courts did not intervene in prison or inmate affairs. This is known as the *hands-off doctrine*.
- The constitutional source of inmate rights include the Eighth Amendment, and the Fourteenth Amendment provisions of due process and equal protection.

Private Prisons
- The first modern private prisons opened in the early 1980s.

- Three companies provide most of the private correctional services in the United States: the Corrections Corporation of America, Wackenhut Corrections Corporation, and Correctional Services Corporation.

Key Terms

argot roles
Specific patterns of behavior that inmates develop in prison in order to adjust to the environment.

hands-off doctrine
The judicial attitude toward prisons prior to the 1960s in which courts did not become involved in prison affairs or inmate rights.

pains of imprisonment
Deprivations that define the punitive nature of imprisonment.

total institution
A closed environment in which every aspect, including the movement and behavior of the people within, is controlled and structured.

Short Answer Questions

Describe how Sykes' pains of imprisonment define the prison experience. Can you think of any additional pains that should be introduced to the prison experience?

_____
_____
_____
_____
_____
_____
_____
_____

Prison gangs are a big problem in some prisons. What could be done to break up the gang structure? Would you be willing to work in a prison that had active and violent gangs?

___

Compare and contrast the Attica and New Mexico prison riots. Which was the most dangerous? Evaluate how the authorities responded to each riot.

___

Describe the various roles of the correctional officer. Which of these job assignments is most attractive?

How have the courts intervened in prison administration? Have the courts gone too far? Do prisoners have too many rights? If you were a prisoner would you think that you had too many rights?

Study Guide Questions

Multiple Choice

1. Inmates' lawyers used these two amendments to convince the courts to reconsider their stance toward prisons.
   a. Second and Fourteenth
   b. Eighth and Fourteenth
   c. Second and Tenth
   d. Fourteenth and Tenth

2. These groups handle inmate situations that might explode into violence or a riot.
   a. Special Operations Response Team
   b. Special Weapons and Tactics Team
   c. Hostile Response Team
   d. Riot Police

3. This Supreme Court decision defined the processes required for prison disciplinary proceedings.
   a. *Terry v. Ohio*
   b. *Hope v. Pelzer*
   c. *Wolff v. McDonnell*
   d. *In re Gault*

4. This is the most prevalent and problematic prison career.
   a. inmate
   b. warden
   c. secretary
   d. correctional officer

5. This is a special language used by prison inmates.
   a. argot
   b. polyglot
   c. slang
   d. patois

6. This case allowed inmates to sue for civil rights violations.
   a. *Wolff v. McDonnell*
   b. *Furman v. Georgia*
   c. *Cooper v. Pate*
   d. *Miranda v. Arizona*

7. Deprivation of liberty and deprivation of security are two
   a. things that happen in prison.
   b. pains of imprisonment.
   c. burdens of incarceration.
   d. conditions of parole.

8. These have replaced many of the classic prison argot roles identified by Gresham Sykes.
   a. separate-and-silent systems
   b. criminological terms
   c. secure housing units
   d. prison gangs

9. Sociologists use this term to explain how the actions of an individual are transmitted into group actions.
   a. bad behavior
   b. riots
   c. social cohesion
   d. collective behavior

10. Here, the inmates' ability to influence the conditions of their confinement is limited.
    a. total institution
    b. hospital
    c. school
    d. halfway institution

True/False

1. Little is required to upset the prison's delicate social system. _____

2. Prison inmates have some legal rights. _____

3. Inmates may use an argot for the various roles they take in order to adapt to imprisonment. _____

4. Prison reform began in the 1930s. _____

5. Discrimination that is prohibited in society may sometimes be permitted in prisons. _____

6. Few prisons are closed institutions where everything is tightly controlled. _____

7. An inmate's cell may be searched without warning. _____

8. "Contact" visits are a constitutional right of prison inmates. _____

9. Prisons may employ many specialist officers. _____

10. There were no differences between the Attica and the New Mexico prison riots. _____

Fill in the Blank

1. "Excessive bail shall not be required, nor excessive fines imposed, nor cruel and unusual punishments inflicted," is from the _____ Amendment.

2. Due process and equal protection are the two clauses of the _____ Amendment that particularly apply to inmates' rights.

3. The _____ is considered the oldest prison gang.

4. _____ prison recalls the separate-and-silent systems in the Pennsylvania and Auburn prisons.

5. In 1980, 33 inmates died in the _____ prison riot.

6. According to the courts' hands-off doctrine, decisions about prisons were considered a matter for the _____ branch, not the judicial.

7. "Allow all New York State prisoners to be politically active, without intimidation or reprisal" was an inmate demand from the _____ prison riot.

8. The case _____ defined the processes required for prison disciplinary proceedings.

9. _____ are correctional officers responsible for the security of a prison's housing block.

10. The first modern _____ prisons opened in the early 1980s.

Find a Flash

Read the two news flashes in Chapter 12 carefully, noting how they illustrate issues covered in the chapter.

- *Mentally Ill Must Go to Prison for Treatment* reviews the criminal justice system's treatment of mentally ill offenders.
- *Bad Food for Bad Behavior* describes the use of food to control unruly inmates.
- *Tough Alabama County Stresses Prisons* looks at a jurisdiction that uses much of its financial resources to support a high incarceration rate.

Use the library or search the web to find two news items that exemplify, explain, or even appear to contradict topics from Chapter 12. Write short summaries of these news items in the spaces provided. If possible, find one local story and one national story. Give your news flashes short titles that explain what they are about. Suggested news flash topics are listed below.

Prison life
Inmate subculture
Prison gangs
Pelican Bay state prison
Prison violence
Prison riots
Attica prison riot
New Mexico prison riot
Working in the prison
Courts and the prison
The Eighth Amendment
The Fourteenth Amendment (due process)
The Fourteenth Amendment (equal protection)
Private prisons

News Flash #1

Title

News Flash #2

Title

What Agency Am I?

Peruse the following descriptions taken from the websites of federal criminal justice-related agencies, programs, and bureaus. Find the organization that matches it in the list and write it in the blank space provided. Hint: Use the web addresses in the list to check the organizations' websites.

A. I seek to employ and provide skills training to the greatest practicable number of inmates confined within the Federal Bureau of Prisons; contribute to the safety and security of the nation's correctional facilities by keeping inmates constructively occupied; produce market-price quality goods for sale to the federal government; operate in a self-sustaining manner; and minimize the agency's impact on private business and labor.

Who Am I? _____

B. I was established September 2001 in response to growing concerns regarding federal detention. I provide for the safe, secure, and humane confinement of persons in federal custody awaiting trial or immigration proceedings by ensuring the appropriate operations and cost effectiveness of secure non-federal detention facilities utilized by federal law enforcement agencies.

Who Am I? _____

C. I provide training, technical assistance, information services, and policy/program development assistance to federal, state, and local corrections agencies. I also provide leadership to influence correctional policies, practices, and operations nationwide in areas of emerging interest and concern to correctional executives and practitioners, as well as public policymakers.

Who Am I? _____

D. I protect society by confining federal offenders in the controlled environments of prisons and community-based facilities that are safe, humane, cost-efficient, and appropriately secure, and that provide work and other self-improvement opportunities to assist offenders in becoming law-abiding citizens.

Who Am I?_____

List

Bureau of Land Management Law Enforcement	http://www.blm.gov/nhp/pubs/brochures/law
Federal Bureau of Prisons	http://www.bop.gov
Federal Prison Industries (UNICOR)	http://www.unicor.gov
National Institute of Corrections	http://nicic.org
Office of the Federal Detention Trustee	http://www.usdoj.gov/ofdt
U.S. Bureau of Industry and Security	http://www.bxa.doc.gov

Word Search

Instructions: Fill in the blanks of the definitions below with the correct word, then find the word in the puzzle!

```
G B X U M P A I N S O F I M P R I S O N M E N T O T S L A F
M F G Y G E A N G Z M S I K C R E T O X I I G F T A K P B E
E C H B F D F R G E U I L P W C Y U F E R J J R J D A A V D
S D A I B R Y D H Z C B S P S J U J Y K S P O W F B C H I N
H W T X E K Z W B A M Q G H M E C M W F N N X P M V K Q G C
V C W N S K G C C D O D Y R G K X N D E B F Q Z U B G Y C A
O B B E Q H L B A U E A C O A P M K V J Z L U N Q J H G A U
C L H R Q J S N E E Y T J A Y R W X J Y P I T P D O S O T O
N V H Y D P E L N P C Y Y M I Z V U U K Y N E G N S T V E T
W N J L O I L Q C R Q J R U C Q B I B S H T L E S O R J M W
I T G H Q H O S W O K R J W R I D J G A O F R G G Z P I O A
L D B D B O R G S C T J U S O D Y X M Z Z H M F J B X U E I
O O L G S I T R T E W F W E I L R K H W J B E T C P R J P R
L G F M Y F O A G S Z Q E S N P B G N K S C U V H J L X B K
D A V J N R G Z M S O N R I P C C H O B Z N H D T Z E E M B
X K T A Y A R J T A Y P S B U R G K Z P U O N J R P J C G L
A O H D I A A L G Q F K U J S L Q O J V S I N P W P L T Z F
C R E Q U A L P R O T E C T I O N C K R X T U N W Y K D K Q
N X V K H O O G K P E R P T Y L K B T P P U P F W J X P Z C
V R G R T S X S X F F O S D N A H U F T S T H X M T G Q H C
W C D X V J J X L Z T J S W L J X K A O I I E T I C K Q M L
P J E O Z Z S P A W K B B L E M J L B P I T P J G A J D Q C
G T I W W N S P E I X D S O L A G J D I Y S Q X Q B D E Y P
E D G Y W A F G M D C I N W P G G A X L O N H S O R K U I X
W L H W B M I G Z S I U B D E A W L R H G I H M O P J Y U O
L F T T Q K V V K O G Y M D K C P W V K B L Z Z D W I P L P
V C H V W D I F D N F C L A S Q W H N J E A G C Q X Y M S D
T F S K E D Y H R T M V Q M Z Y H R X D Q T V Q C T W U H M
H J I X G A J C B C O E S K D D L X G B T O V Q I A J S B L
B I L E H J T I J N W I D B T V Z O K X N T P R T R M R Y L
```

Definitions

1. _____ are specific patterns of behavior that inmates develop in prison in order to adjust to the environment.

2. The _____ doctrine describes the judicial attitude toward prisons prior to the 1960s in which courts did not become involved in prison affairs or inmate rights.

3. Deprivations that define the punitive nature of imprisonment are called the _____.

4. A closed environment in which every aspect, including the movement and behavior of the people within, is controlled and structured is called a _____.

5. "Excessive bail shall not be required, nor excessive fines imposed, nor cruel and unusual punishments inflicted" is the text of the _____ Amendment.

6. The rights of _____ and _____ are described in the Fourteenth Amendment.

Chapter 13
Corrections in the Community

Learning Objectives
After reading this chapter, you should be able to:

1. Describe the four community corrections strategies.
2. Discuss the purpose of community corrections and why every offender does not go to jail or prison.
3. Discuss the purpose of diversion and arguments for and against it.
4. Discuss probation and arguments for and against it.
5. Describe how each of the participants in the criminal justice process views probation.
6. Understand the probation officer's job.
7. Discuss parole and arguments for and against it.
8. Discuss intermediate sanctions and arguments for and against using them.
9. Compare and contrast shock probation and boot camp prisons.
10. Discuss the purpose of jails.

Chapter Summary and Key Concepts
Chapter 13 reviews alternatives to prison for criminal offenders; these include probation (*instead* of prison) and parole (*after* prison).

Community Corrections and Diversion
- Society cannot afford to imprison everyone who violates the law. Community corrections are a way to punish offenders without incarcerating them.
- Prisons only achieve the goals of incapacitation, retribution, and rehabilitation in a limited manner.
- The four interrelated community corrections strategies are: diversion programs, probation, parole, and intermediate sanctions.
- Offenders may be sent to alternative programs at several junctures in the criminal justice system.
- Diversion programs are popular for first-time offenders who have committed minor offenses.

Probation
- Probation is a widely used sentencing alternative in which offenders are not incarcerated if they promise good behavior and agree to restrictions and/or requirements set by a judge.
- There are more probationers than inmates or parolees, and state probationers outnumber federal probationers.
- Three activities define the occupation of the probation officer: investigation, supervision, and service.
- The probation officer is responsible for writing the presentence investigation report.

- The presentence investigation report contains information about two important aspects of the case: the legal history of the incident and the offender's social history.

Parole
- Parole is for offenders who are leaving prison after serving a partial sentence.
- Parole grew from the philosophy that the penal system should help the offender return to society.
- Parolees face much of the same restrictions and requirements as probationers.
- The decision to grant parole is based on three principles: retribution, rehabilitation, and prison space.
- Parole boards make their decisions based on time served, prison adjustment, pre-parole plan, offender interview, and victim-impact statements.
- Offenders returning to society face three primary obstacles: prisonization, weakened social ties, and stigmatization.

Intermediate Sanctions
- Intermediate sanctions are sentencing alternatives that exist between probation and incarceration. Notable examples are intensive supervision probation, drug testing, house arrest/electronic monitoring, fines, and boot-camp prisons.
- Shock probation is a program in which the offender receives a false sentence in jail or prison, but is released on probation after 30 to 90 days of incarceration.

Jails
- Jails are fundamental to the corrections system.
- Jails hold suspects awaiting disposition and misdemeanor offenders sentenced to less than a year of incarceration.
- The local jail may be connected to a larger local corrections system that includes work-release programs, road crews, stockades, and local probation departments.
- Jails are controlled by either the local sheriff or a jail administrator.

Key Terms

boot-camp prison
A short-term prison that uses military boot-camp training and discipline techniques to rehabilitate offenders. Often used for young offenders.

good time
The time deducted from an inmate's prison sentence for good behavior.

intensive supervision probation
A form of supervision that requires frequent meetings between the client and probation officer(s).

master status
A personal status that overwhelms all others. For example, "rapist" obliterates a positive status such as "good student" or "sports star."

meritorious time
Time deducted from an inmate's sentence for doing something special or extra, such as getting a GED.

presentence investigation
The report prepared by a probation officer to assist a judge in sentencing. The report usually contains information about the offender's arrests, prior convictions, work history, and family. May also be called "presentencing report."

shock probation
The practice of sentencing offenders to prison, allowing them to serve a short time, then granting them probation without their prior knowledge.

Short Answer Questions

What are the multiple goals of the criminal justice system? Which of these goals is community corrections best able to address?

_____
_____
_____
_____
_____
_____
_____
_____
_____
_____
_____

What is the difference between probation and parole? Are the clients of one system inherently more dangerous than the other? Would you rather be a probation officer or a parole officer?

_____

What factors are taken into consideration when authorities decide to parole an inmate? Do you think the victim of the crime should have any input in the decision to grant parole?

_____

What obstacles do inmates confront when they try to re-enter society? What can the parole officer do to help the parolee handle these difficulties?

What are intermediate punishments? Are they a good use of the limited money available for corrections? Which of these intermediate punishments seems the most beneficial to you?

Study Guide Questions

Multiple Choice

1. A probation officer who suspects criminal activity does not need this Fourth Amendment provision to search a probationer's residence, car, or person.
a. probable cause
b. Miranda warning
c. police officer
d. reasonable doubt

2. In this case, the Supreme Court stated that felony defendants must be allowed an attorney during hearings when probation may be revoked or a deferred sentence imposed.
a. *Miranda v. Arizona*
b. *Howard v. Fine*
c. *Mempa v. Rhay*
d. *Morrissey v. Brewer*

3. The probation officer investigates the offender's
a. legal history and school records.
b. legal history and social history.
c. social history and financial history.
d. medical history and school records.

4. In order to ensure adequate supervision, dangerous probationers may be placed
a. on intensive supervision probation.
b. on regular probation.
c. in jail.
d. in a therapeutic environment.

5. These three activities define the probation officer's job.
a. incapacitation; supervision; service
b. investigation; retribution; socialization
c. incapacitation; retribution; service
d. investigation; supervision; service

6. In this case, the Supreme Court provided minimum due process requirements for the revocation of parole.
a. *Hope v. Pelzer*
b. *Morrissey v. Brewer*
c. *Terry v. Ohio*
d. *Mempa v. Rhay*

7. Diversion programs are based on this theory.
a. XYY theory
b. strain theory

c. labeling theory
d. broken windows theory

8. Inmates may be granted this for behaving in prison, which can significantly reduce their sentences.
a. overtime
b. time served
c. meritorious time
d. good time

9. The multiple goals of the criminal justice system are
a. incapacitation, retribution, and rehabilitation.
b. indoctrination, retribution, and socialization.
c. insubordination, contribution, and rehabilitation.
d. incapacitation, retribution, and socialization.

10. These are two of the obstacles that inmates face when returning to society.
a. alienation and stigmatization
b. prisonization and stigmatization
c. alienation and socialization
d. prisonization and socialization

True/False

1. The determination of probation risk is a legal issue in which offenders are protected by the court and is not the responsibility of probation departments. _____

2. Intermediate punishments are used only for felons. _____

3. Probation officers are able to ensure that all the conditions of probation are being followed at all times. _____

4. All violations of the technical conditions of probation do not result in revocation of probation. _____

5. Everyone who violates the law is incarcerated. _____

6. Fines are sometimes combined with other types of sanctions. _____

7. Criminal cases are usually settled by plea bargaining. _____

8. Offenders may be diverted to alternative programs at a number of points in the criminal justice system. _____

9. Jails are a little-used part of the criminal justice system. _____

10. There are more offenders on probation than in prison or on parole. _____

Fill in the Blank

1. Probation _____, parole _____.

2. The release of an inmate who has received a long prison sentence after serving only a short period of time is called _____.

3. Electronic monitoring is a(n) _____ sanction.

4. _____ hold suspects awaiting disposition and misdemeanor offenders.

5. A former inmate's _____ status may present a formidable obstacle to re-entering society.

6. The _____ is good at achieving the goal of incapacitation.

7. The number of inmates who successfully complete parole is about _____ of them.

8. Reduced-caseload strategies that ensure that problematic probationers receive more attention are called _____.

9. _____ is a sentence that is less expensive than prison and satisfies society somewhat that the offender has been punished.

10. The _____ is prepared by a probation officer to assist a judge in sentencing.

Find a Flash

Read the news flash in Chapter 13 carefully, noting how it illustrates issues covered in the chapter.

- *Throwing Away the Key* explores how sex offenders may serve extra time by being committed to mental institutions after they have served their prison sentences.

Use the library or search the web to find two news items that exemplify, explain, or even appear to contradict topics from Chapter 13. Write short summaries of these news items in the spaces provided. If possible, find one local story and one national story. Give your news flashes short titles that explain what they are about. Suggested news flash topics are listed below.

Diversion	Probation
Parole	Probation and/or parole officers
Intermediate sanctions	Boot-camp prisons
Shock probation	Jails

News Flash #1

Title

News Flash #2

Title

What Agency Am I?

Peruse the following descriptions taken from the websites of federal criminal justice-related agencies, programs, and bureaus. Find the organization that matches it in the list and write it in the blank space provided. Hint: Use the web addresses in the list to check the organizations' websites.

A. I promote public safety and strive for justice and fairness in the release and supervision of offenders under my jurisdiction. My guiding principle is to apply the least restrictive sanction that is consistent with public safety and the appropriate punishment of the offense. In making my determinations, I consider information from a variety of sources, including the pre-sentence report, victim of the offense, sentencing judge, prosecutor, defense attorney, prison officials, and offender. I have jurisdiction over federal offenders, D.C. code offenders, Uniform Code of Military Justice offenders, transfer-treaty cases, and state probationers and parolees in the Federal Witness Protection Program.

Who Am I? _____

B. I am a Department of Education office that provides technical assistance to states, local schools, and correctional institutions and shares information on correctional education. One of my duties is to collect information on the number of individuals who complete a vocational education sequence, earn a high school degree or general equivalency diploma, or earn a postsecondary degree while incarcerated.

Who Am I? _____

C. Part of the National Institute of Justice, I offer support, research findings, and technological expertise to help state and local law enforcement and corrections personnel perform their duties more safely and efficiently.

Who Am I? _____

List

Bureau of Land Management Law Enforcement	http://www.blm.gov/nhp/pubs/brochures/law
Federal Judicial Center	http://www.fjc.gov
National Law Enforcement and Corrections Technology Center	http://www.nlectc.org
Office of Correctional Education	http://www.ed.gov/offices/OVAE/AdultEd/OCE
Office of the Pardon Attorney	http://www.usdoj.gov/pardon
U.S. Parole Commission	http://www.usdoj.gov/uspc
U.S. Sentencing Commission	http://www.ussc.gov

Word Search

Instructions: Fill in the blanks of the definitions below with the correct word, then find the word in the puzzle!

```
F R K T M P R E S E N T E N C E I N V E S T I G A T I O N P
M O J M S Z P L S Y A F N N L O Z V W V M N A U A L V X E F
J L S K S B Y F E J D L X O A W U V I G I E E D Z A E K D O
U J A P S P J D M R N E I A A O V V M A V G W J N X E U R S
W I B L N H S C I G N S G H Z Z M A B K R S H U Q A C V M U
A R U C M P V F T Y N L V B L L S Q R S C E P L G B J I Z R
W R Y X Y B W F D D M X J Z L T S O V A R C B D Z H P P Z R
K K J O G O Y U O F Z B N Z E T U X Q M O J J Q L C W J F D
X I H V Q X C B O G L L I R Y G R W B Q N K B F Q T H U J Y
M J J W R E D I G T N F S Q X L X S P U D H J U X T J M V L
Q J Y Z I A V N S T V T D A O U L P V G R Y C H R E N H K I
H B Q I Y F E T M U A N O S I R P P M A C T O O B I I G I T
F W B Z W R P E X T J C J B N G J P W L U P A G F K V E F P
V A Q Y D R V N U R B A Q I M H V P J M W V I E S K K R K G
I Q L P F N V S U C A Q P C D A M Y R X K Z U Z X V O W O O
I D W Y N R J I T C E L V B V Z U S D N F K N Z S C T N L G
C U Y Q B V L V E M I T S U O I R O T I R E M T O G H Z Q A
P Q W D R G T E W S F X S W G H N V Q X K K G I D C T N D H
E I I O R K B S H K M Q K C N L I Y C Q D I H E E R S Y G T
T C O Q W J Z U B Z F Y F V E O Y O V W N L L D M I Y S E J
N J K Y Z E P P U N N O I T A B O R P K C O H S C D K R Y J
S Z H U M R E E V S W D C Q I D F M P R K E C X G F W K L X
C H T O R J A R E M J W E W W M C H R S M Q I D Y Q L I K T
W P X E W J R V I O R Z T Z L M M A S C M H M F B Z R Y T W
F X I O M L A I A V I V B I J A V V S L C R Y S R R S E Y T
H X M X V G B S S F V Q O C X F C V O Y E Z T R W A F H L P
Q X Z N X S O I X L O I N T O B Y P M I B B V E U Y B L G T
U I O J F A O O O V S J Y H S P Q U S R W U G H Y M K Y N G
W W U H D C S N H B H Q L I S X D U X H S T T T Z O G Q R P
A W M B S L L Q O K I G I O X J G S H R S W B R X A T V Z M
```

Definitions

1. A _____ is a short-term facility that uses military-style training and discipline techniques to rehabilitate offenders.

2. The period deducted from an inmate's prison sentence for good behavior is called _____.

3. _____ probation requires frequent meetings between the client and probation officer(s).

4. A _____ is a personal status that overwhelms all others.

5. _____ is deducted from an inmate's sentence for doing something special or extra, such as getting a GED.

6. The _____ report is prepared by a probation officer to assist a judge in sentencing.

7. _____ is the practice of sentencing offenders to prison, allowing them to serve a short time, then granting them probation without their prior knowledge.

Match the Case

Part Four
From Penology to Corrections and Back

Draw a line from the case to its outcome.

Cooper v. Pate	This decision established limits for the execution of the mentally retarded.
Mempa v. Rhay	This case helped set guidelines for what constitutes cruel and unusual punishment in prison and the circumstances under which prison officials are liable.
Hope v. Pelzer	This decision banned execution of the insane.
Wolff v. McDonnell	This case helped end the judicial "hands-off" doctrine toward prisons by allowing inmates to sue for civil-rights violations.
Ford v. Wainwright	The U.S. Supreme Court provided minimum due process requirements for the revocation of parole.
Atkins v. Virginia	This case defined the processes required for prison disciplinary proceedings.
Morrissey v. Brewer	Felony defendants must be allowed to have an attorney during hearings when probation may be revoked or a deferred sentence imposed.

Chapter 14
Juvenile Delinquency and Juvenile Justice

Learning Objectives
After reading this chapter, students should be able to:

1. Understand why the modern criminal justice system treats young offenders differently than adult offenders.
2. Understand the position and role of children in pre-20th century times.
3. Discuss the concept of *parens patriae*.
4. Describe the purpose of houses of refuge.
5. Understand the problems of the child-saving movement.
6. Describe the reforms in juvenile justice at the beginning of the 20th century.
7. Discuss the categories of children who most often come in contact with the juvenile justice system.
8. Discuss the societal issues that can cause children to come in contact with the juvenile justice system.
9. Describe the general structure of the juvenile justice system.
10. Discuss positive and negative trends that may affect the delinquency of children in the future.

Chapter Summary and Key Concepts
Chapter 14 presents a brief history of the treatment of young people and examines youth crime and the juvenile justice system.

The History of Society and Children
- Not all ancient societies treated children the same way. In early England, the authority for dealing with children resided with the parents and not the state.
- In early England the concept of *parens patriae* meant that the king could intervene in the interests of children.
- In colonial America, no special system existed for juvenile offenders, and parents were responsible for their children's actions.
- The first house of refuge was established in New York City in 1825. Other states designed similar types of institutions over the next 60 years.
- A major 20th-century reform was the removal of responsibility for children from the adult criminal court.
- In 1899, the first juvenile court was established in Cook County, Illinois.

Modern Society and Children
- Some of the most pressing issues facing young people include violence, alcohol and drugs, sex and sexual abuse, running away, depression, and nihilism.
- Societal institutions and issues connected to the problem of juvenile crime include school quality, poverty, faulty families, and neighborhood quality.

- Trends that may influence how society deals with juveniles are a growing elderly population, the privatization of youth programs, the continuing transfer of juveniles to adult criminal courts, and the increasing age of child dependency.

The Juvenile Justice System
- The juvenile justice system is responsible for children who are incorrigible, dependent, neglected, delinquent, and/or status offenders.
- The juvenile justice system has its own philosophy, courts, and correctional system.
- The major differences between juvenile court and adult court are focus on rehabilitation, informal and private hearings, and individualized justice.
- The stages of the juvenile justice system are entry via referral, pre-hearing detention, intake, determining jurisdiction, the adjudication hearing, the disposition, and aftercare.
- Four types of public facilities for juveniles are available in many states: adult prisons, ranches and camps, boot-camp prisons, and traditional training schools.

Key Terms

adjudicatory hearing
The process in which a juvenile court determines if the allegations in a petition are supported by evidence.

adversarial process
A term describing the manner in which U.S. criminal trial courts operate; a system that requires two sides, a prosecution and a defense.

chancery court
"Court of equity." In England, these were established, in part, to assist in dispensing justice when common law courts failed to resolve a case. These courts were favorable to vulnerable individuals, especially children.

commitment
An order by a judge upon conviction or before a trial that sends a person to jail or prison. Also, a judge's order that sends a mentally unstable person to a mental institution.

consent decree
When the parties to a lawsuit accept a judge's order that is based upon an agreement made by them instead of continuing the case through a trial or hearing.

due process rights
Guarantees by the Fifth, Sixth, and Fourteenth Amendments of the U.S. Constitution establishing legal procedures that recognize the protection of an individual's life, liberty, and property.

gatekeeping
At several points throughout the juvenile justice process, officials make important decisions that determine what happens to the youth. Examples of these decision points or "gates" are the

prosecutor's determination of whether to charge the youth with a crime and the judge's decision to sentence the youth to probation or detention.

hearing
A session that takes place without a jury before a judge or magistrate in which evidence and/or argument is presented to determine some factual or legal issue.

indentured servant
From the 17th to 19th centuries, a person who came to the American colonies/United States and was made to work for a period of time, usually seven years.

informal probation
A period during which a juvenile is required to stay out of trouble or make restitution before the case is dropped.

juvenile delinquent
A person, usually under the age of 18, who is determined to have committed a crime or status offense in states in which a minor is declared to lack responsibility and who cannot be sentenced as an adult.

parens patriae
Latin for "father of the country." Refers to the philosophy that the government is the ultimate guardian of all children or disabled adults.

petitioner
A person who files a lawsuit; also called a "plaintiff."

poor laws
Seventeenth-century laws that turned over vagrants and abandoned children to land-owners or shopkeepers as indentured servants.

referral
Similar to a "charge" in the adult system in which an authority, usually police, parents, or the school, determines that the youth needs intervention from the juvenile court.

residential placement
Any sentence of a juvenile offender to a halfway house or other community home in which the juvenile is closely monitored, but allowed to leave for work or school.

respondent
The party who must reply to a petitioner's complaint. Equivalent to a defendant in a lawsuit.

status offense
An act that is considered a legal offense only when committed by a juvenile and that can be adjudicated only in a juvenile court.

statutory exclusion
Provisions that exclude, without hearing or waiver, juveniles who meet certain age, offense, or past record criteria from the jurisdiction of the juvenile court. Excluded juvenile offenders are automatically tried in adult criminal court. Crimes that would invoke statutory exclusion may include murder, aggravated rape, and armed robbery.

zero-tolerance policies
Policies of agencies in which the strict letter of the law or rule is followed without question or room for individual discretion on the part of the authority.

Short Answer Questions

What are the differences between childhood today and childhood in earlier times? Were children always treated as well as they are today?

What are the major court cases that have advanced the rights of juveniles? Have these cases gone too far in protecting young offenders from the law?

How is juvenile crime related to other institutions? Can reform in other areas of society affect the prevalence and seriousness of juvenile delinquency?

How do the proceedings of the juvenile court differ from the adult criminal court? Describe how the different philosophies of the courts are translated into protections of legal rights.

What do you see as the most pressing issues in juvenile justice today? Has the time come to abandon the juvenile justice system and treat young offenders the same way we treat adult offenders?

Study Guide Questions

Multiple Choice

1. These are behaviors that are considered legitimate for adults, but deviant if committed by children.
   a. age-related offenses
   b. juvenile offenses
   c. misdemeanors
   d. status offenses

2. Two parties to a lawsuit decide to make an agreement instead of continuing the case through a trial and accept a judge's order based upon this agreement. This is called a
   a. judicial decree.
   b. interlocutory decree.
   c. final decree.
   d. consent decree.

3. This case set forth that a case against a juvenile must be proved beyond a reasonable doubt if incarceration or loss of freedom is possible.
   a. *In re Winship*
   b. *In re Gault*
   c. *Kent v. United States*
   d. *Schall v. Martin*

4. This allows a juvenile's case to be diverted without formal charges as long as the juvenile meets prescribed conditions.
   a. juvenile probation
   b. informal parole
   c. shock probation
   d. informal probation

5. Established in New York City in the 19th century, _____ were intended to provide education and protection for delinquent children.
   a. halfway houses
   b. houses of refuge
   c. orphanages
   d. reformatories

6. Although not considered a criminal proceeding, this is the equivalent of a trial in the adult criminal court.
   a. juvenile hearing
   b. adjudicatory trial
   c. adjudicatory hearing
   d. juvenile trial

7. This is when a judge sends a juvenile to adult court.
a. legislative waiver
b. direct filing
c. mandatory waiver
d. judicial waiver

8. This concept established the government's protection of children's welfare.
a. *parens patriae*
b. *lex talionis*
c. *voir dire*
d. *mens rea*

9. This boosted the status of children in England.
a. transportation
b. workhouses
c. poor laws
d. boot-camp prisons

10. Legally, a child who has committed a crime is called a
a. bad kid.
b. juvenile delinquent.
c. pre-adult offender.
d. minor.

True/False

1. Juveniles never go to adult prisons. _____

2. The juvenile court system may share personnel with the adult court system. _____

3. The juvenile justice system has little or no focus on rehabilitation. _____

4. Juvenile court decisions may affect entire families. _____

5. Some youths convicted of crimes go to boot-camp prisons. _____

6. Juveniles are never diverted from the justice system. _____

7. There are no major differences between adult criminal court and juvenile court. _____

8. Each state has its own structure and method of processing juvenile justice cases. _____

9. In an adjudicatory hearing, the judge also acts as jury. _____

10. As far as the criminal justice system is concerned, children may do whatever adults do. _____

Fill in the Blank

1. Using _____, a prosecutor may file charges in either juvenile or adult court.

2. _____ policies are those in which the strict letter of the law is followed without discretion.

3. Cases are inserted into the juvenile justice system via _____.

4. The prosecutor in a juvenile hearing is called a _____.

5. The Supreme Court ruled in _____ that a juvenile's due process rights are denied when his or her case is waived to adult criminal court without a formal hearing.

6. The _____ process is not a feature of the juvenile adjudicatory hearing.

7. The defense attorney in a juvenile hearing is called a _____.

8. Despite the differences in the adult and juvenile criminal justice systems, both juveniles and adults have the right to a(n) _____ and protection against _____.

9. As set forth by the case _____, detention of a juvenile is constitutional if it protects the juvenile and society from crimes he or she may commit pre-trial.

10. In 1899, the first juvenile court was established in _____.

Find a Flash

Read the news flash in Chapter 14 carefully, noting how it illustrates issues covered in the chapter.

- *(Il)legal Fiction* reviews the effect of school shootings on zero-tolerance policies.

Use the library or search the web to find two news items that exemplify, explain, or even appear to contradict topics from Chapter 14. Write short summaries of these news items in the spaces provided. If possible, find one local story and one national story. Give your news flashes short titles that explain what they are about. Suggested news flash topics are listed below.

The juvenile justice system
Conditions of youth confinement
Zero tolerance

Youth gangs
Treating children as adults
The future of juvenile justice

News Flash #1

Title

News Flash #2

Title

What Agency Am I?

Peruse the following descriptions taken from the websites of federal criminal justice-related agencies, programs, and bureaus. Find the organization that matches it in the list and write it in the blank space provided. Hint: Use the web addresses in the list to check the organizations' websites.

A. I am a Health and Human Services agency that funds state, territory, local, and tribal organizations to provide family assistance, child support, child care, Head Start, child welfare, and other programs relating to children and families.

Who Am I? _____

B. I foster coordination, collaboration, and integration of collection and reporting of federal data on child and family issues and conditions. I develop priorities for collecting enhanced data on children and youth, and improve the reporting and dissemination of information on the status of children to the policy community and the general public.

Who Am I? _____

C. I provide national leadership, coordination, and resources to prevent and respond to juvenile delinquency and victimization. I support states and communities in developing and implementing effective and coordinated prevention and intervention programs and improving the juvenile justice system so that it protects public safety, holds offenders accountable, and provides treatment and rehabilitative services tailored to the needs of juveniles and their families.

Who Am I? _____

List

Administration for Children and Families	http://www.acf.hhs.gov
Federal Interagency Forum on Child and Family Statistics	http://www.childstats.gov
Federal Judicial Center	http://www.fjc.gov
Office of Correctional Education	http://www.ed.gov/offices/OVAE/AdultEd/OCE
Office of Juvenile Justice and Delinquency Prevention	http://ojjdp.ncjrs.org
Office of the Pardon Attorney	http://www.usdoj.gov/pardon
U.S. Sentencing Commission	http://www.ussc.gov

Word Search

Instructions: Fill in the blanks of the definitions below with the correct word, then find the word in the puzzle!

```
W A L T N E M T I M M O C E T I U R E S P O N D E N T R Z O
G K B L Q R Y P N P D N S V L D E S A Z B G Z O H K I J J I
N A L K Z N O N J F G M S S S G D T M N X L F J Y C G H H
I W I N Z C D D E X L Z C P M G J U E G K F C S R Z D L K X
P V G H U I A H F F U A H N Q U D P U V T H Z E Q T Q L O Q
E N F N M L Y Z V Y R O T Z D O N I U M X F C N C M E W I R
E M Y D I O E S P P Z K O I D C D I L B K N Y I T C R Y P R
K J J S E R Z V S A A C C L R E F E R R A L V F D Z V B E P
E I V R A O A N B Q R A Y X F X Q A J H C X M S G D I S V S
T A H S Q G V E T B T R J V I X P H C F I K V P J L I J B R
A B T X A J E X H O O F F K G D L N D Z H C N D P D J F X G
G K N G N K H P R T L S S Q S A H C H I H O I P E Y G E A V
A Z A D F T N Y U F V N F F I Z L T Q R I N A N T Z Q B T F
P M V E R W O T H Q G J A R Q W N J B T W O T K E D Q C B P
O B R A G C A Q E N G V A L Q V Z O A J T I J B G Q D S P D
O I E N S T V G O L U S A V L Q U B V S A A U C G D V E T B
R Z S H S S S E C O R P E U D U O G U L S Z S M Z A T P E J
L P D V P T P O W E V P H S D R D N Q O L L J O Y B E F X I
A J E S W Y Y R V A M I Y Y P Y O G C T N V Y T X N T O I N
W I R F D U Q D S L T N E U Q N I L E D E L I N E V U J K T
S S U H W P A V X T C U P L S U S G J Y S N I C U Q P V Z U
V X T F U D V N D T P D V T V V X R B J N J L R P R S K I
I T N G S L R N R I A Z C O N S E N T D E C R E E U U Q C Y
S P E I R E N V F S W P A R E N S P A T R I A E K T P D F M
T T D H F T U A E E R E L T Y F C X V J K Q A I C B G T K L
F D N F Q V F R E N O I T I T E P H X E P U K A K H U R R M
K F I X P C R I Z S T A T U S O F F E N S E K S E R O V L P
A M F H C Q P J K P L L C L C T H U R G O N H K R V G T D E
L I J V M I D X B R O E N G T J Q R E I H D P H D N F H D U
J U G O Z Q S S W U D Z X X V F Q Y F D P X B Q B O S M V Y
```

Definitions

1. During the _____ hearing a juvenile court determines if the allegations in a petition are supported by evidence.

2. The _____ process describes the manner in which U.S. criminal trial courts operate, a system that requires two sides, a prosecution and a defense.

3. _____ court is also known as the "court of equity."

4. A _____ is a judge's order upon conviction or before trial that sends a person to jail or prison.

5. A _____ is reached when the parties to a lawsuit accept a judge's order that is based upon an agreement made by them instead of continuing the case through trial or hearing.

6. _____ rights are guarantees by the Fifth, Sixth, and Fourteenth Amendments of the U.S. Constitution establishing legal procedures that recognize the protection of an individual's life, liberty, and property.

7. _____ describes points throughout the juvenile justice process in which important decisions are made by officials who determine what happens to a youth.

8. A _____ is a session that takes place without a jury before a judge or magistrate in which evidence and/or argument is presented to determine some factual or legal issue.

9. From the 17th to 19th centuries, a person who came to the American colonies/United States and was made to work for a period of time was an _____.

10. An informal _____ period is one in which a youth must stay out of trouble or make restitution before a case is dropped.

11. A person under a certain age (usually 18) who has committed a crime or status offense is called a _____.

12. _____ refers to the philosophy that the government is the ultimate guardian of all children or disabled adults.

13. A _____ is someone who files a lawsuit.

14. _____ were 17th-century legislation that turned over vagrants and abandoned children to land-owners or shopkeepers as indentured servants.

15. A _____ is similar to a "charge" in the adult system.

16. A sentence of a juvenile offender to a halfway house or other community home in which the juvenile is closely monitored, but allowed to leave for work or school, is known as _____ placement.

17. A _____ must reply to a petitioner's complaint.

18. A _____ is considered against the law only when committed by a juvenile.

19. _____ exclusion describes provisions that exclude, without hearing or waiver, juveniles who meet certain age, offense, or past record criteria from the jurisdiction of the juvenile court.

Chapter 15
Crime and Values: Drugs, Gambling, and Sex Work

Learning Objectives
After reading this chapter, you should be able to:

1. Discuss why drug use, gambling, and sex work are controversial issues.
2. Explain the concept of victimless crimes.
3. Describe a brief history of drug use in the United States.
4. Discuss why Prohibition was a failure.
5. Discuss the concept of a war on drugs.
6. Discuss the criminal justice system's attempt to treat drug addicts.
7. Compare and contrast arguments for and against drug legalization and/or decriminalization.
8. Discuss why some forms of gambling are legal and sanctioned by the state, whereas other forms are not.
9. Compare and contrast illegal prostitution and legalized prostitution.
10. Discuss the fact that gambling and prostitution exist in a legal and social gray area, in which some forms of these activities are illegal and others are not.

Chapter Summary and Key Concepts
Chapter 15 examines the influence that drug use, illegal gambling, and prostitution exert on the criminal justice system and their popular status as victimless crimes.

Drugs
- The first popular drug in the United States was alcohol.
- The 1791 Whiskey Rebellion was provoked by a whiskey tax opposed by farmers who believed the government could not tax the states.
- Opium, morphine, and cocaine were legal in the late 1800s and used as ingredients in many patent medicines.
- The Pure Food and Drug Act of 1906 required food and drug sellers to label what their products contained, but did not criminalize drugs.
- The 1914 Harrison Act imposed a tax on opium and cocaine.
- The ratification of the Eighteenth Amendment (or Volstead Act) in 1919 prohibited the use and sale of alcohol. Prohibition ended in 1933.
- In 1937, the government began to control the use and sale of marijuana.
- The 1951 Boggs Act increased penalties for violating drug laws and regulated both narcotics and marijuana. The 1956 Narcotics Control Act increased penalties and federal authority.
- The Controlled Substances Act of 1970 produced the drug schedules currently used to classify drugs.
- The criminal justice system approaches drug control from both a legal and medical perspective. It is illegal to possess and distribute certain drugs, but it is not illegal to be an addict.

- Drug legalization refers to the total removal of legal prohibitions on the possession, use, and sale of certain drugs. Drug decriminalization refers to a reduction in penalties for these acts.

Gambling
- Some states and communities allow almost any form of gambling, while others are more restrictive.
- Many states operate lotteries to raise funds.
- Internet-based gambling has caused problems as some sites are located outside the United States, and the government cannot collect taxes or regulate it.

Sex Work
- Three types of controversial sexual behaviors involve the selling of sex: prostitution, pornography, and exotic dancing. These represent either crimes of values or economic crimes in which the government is unable to set standards, regulate access, and/or impose taxes.
- According to N. Jane McCandless, the four-level occupational hierarchy of prostitution is call girls, exotic dancers, those who engage in prostitution from brothels, and those who engage in prostitution from the street.
- Some prostitutes are male.
- Prostitution is illegal in every U.S. jurisdiction with the exception of state-licensed brothels in Nevada.
- The exact definition of pornography is open to interpretation. Each community or jurisdiction sets its own standards as to what is considered pornography.

Key Terms

community standards
Practices, acts, and/or media accepted by a given social group that shares a geographic area and/or government.

decriminalization
The emendation of laws or statutes to lessen or remove penalties for specific acts subject to criminal prosecution, arrest, and imprisonment.

legalization
The total removal of legal prohibitions on specific acts that were previously proscribed and punishable by law.

sex work
The exchange of coital or sex-related activities for payment.

victimless crimes
Behaviors such as gambling or prostitution that are deemed undesirable because they offend community standards rather than directly harm people or property.

Short Answer Questions

Exactly what are victimless crimes? Don't "victimless crimes" have at least indirect victims? Is it the legitimate role of the government to protect us from ourselves?

Early drug control was aimed at ensuring that the government received taxes for drug transactions. Describe how the philosophy of the government has changed over the years.

Has the war on drugs been successful? Describe the positive and negative aspects of waging such a war on ourselves. What is your opinion of drug legalization? Decriminalization?

Gambling laws have changed greatly in recent years. What role should government play in allowing or regulating gambling? Is legalized gambling simply a tax on those who do not understand odds?

Sexual behavior is a very private matter that has long been regulated by the government. Describe some current issues concerning the intersections of sex and the government.

Study Guide Questions

Multiple Choice

1. This required food and drug makers to clearly label the contents of their products.
   a. Pure Food and Drug Act of 1906
   b. Harrison Act of 1914
   c. Pure Food and Drug Act of 1916
   d. Labeled Contents Act of 1920

2. The drug schedules currently used to classify drugs come from this.
   a. Controlled Substances Act of 1990
   b. Marijuana Tax Act of 1970
   c. Harrison Act of 1990
   d. Controlled Substances Act of 1970

3. This term describes the total removal of prohibitions on acts that were previously illegal.
   a. decriminalization
   b. legalization
   c. repeal
   d. uncriminalization

4. Drug use, illegal gambling, and prostitution are considered by many to be
a. victimless crimes.
b. immoral.
c. illegal.
d. felonies.

5. These are licensed by the state in Nevada, the only state that does so.
a. brothels
b. bars
c. strip clubs
d. methadone clinics

6. This ensured that the government collected taxes from drug-sellers.
a. Marijuana Tax Act
b. Pure Food and Drug Act
c. Harrison Act
d. Whiskey Tax Act

7. The Supreme Court set forth a new three-part test for obscenity in this case.
a. *Jacobellis v. Ohio*
b. *Miller v. California*
c. *Terry v. Ohio*
d. *U.S. v. Flynt*

8. This provoked the 1791 Whiskey Rebellion.
a. a tax on whiskey passed by the English government
b. a shortage of corn
c. too much whiskey
d. a tax on whiskey passed by Congress

9. The Volstead Act was also known as this.
a. the Marijuana Tax Act
b. the National Prohibition Act
c. the Omnibus Crime Control Bill
d. The Fourteenth Amendment

10. These contained a lot of alcohol as well as cocaine and morphine.
a. mixed drinks
b. soda pop
c. patent medicines
d. sleeping pills

True/False

1. Gambling has become legal in some form in almost every state. _____

2. Crimes that involve assault are crimes of values. _____

3. With prostitution, there is always a victim to alert law enforcement. _____

4. It is illegal to be a drug addict. _____

5. Prostitution is not strictly defined as involving a female prostitute and male customer. _____

6. Laws that regulate exotic dancing vary across jurisdictions. _____

7. The move to control drugs in the United States began in the early 20th century. _____

8. What is obscene is very clearly defined and specified by the law. _____

9. Jurisdictions control whether pornography is sold in local stores. _____

10. Early Americans avoided alcohol and stuck to water. _____

Fill in the Blank

1. "I know it when I see it," was Justice Potter Stewart's definition of pornography in the case _____.

2. During the Civil War, _____ was used to combat pain and dysentery.

3. The 1951 _____ Act increased penalties for violating drug laws.

4. According to N. Jane McCandless, the top level in the hierarchy of prostitution is the _____ or _____.

5. Prohibition began with the passage of the _____ Amendment in 1919. It ended with the passage of the _____ Amendment.

6. The case _____ demonstrates the movement of a controversial activity, prostitution, from extra-legal toleration into a state's legal code.

7. The ban on the manufacture, sale, and transportation of alcohol was repealed in _____.

8. The 1956 _____ increased penalties and federal authority for drug crimes.

9. The United States legal system relies on the _____ guideline to define obscenity.

10. The emendation of laws to lessen or remove penalties for illegal acts is called _____.

Find a Flash
Read the two news flashes in Chapter 15 carefully, noting how they illustrate issues covered in the chapter.

- *Gambling in Your Pajamas* reviews Internet gambling and the challenges it has presented to law enforcement.
- *Police Target "Houses of Ill-Repute"* assesses prostitution stings.

Use the library or search the web to find two news items that exemplify, explain, or even appear to contradict topics from Chapter 15. Write short summaries of these news items in the spaces provided. If possible, find one local story and one national story. Give your news flashes short titles that explain what they are about. Suggested news flash topics are listed below.

Drug abuse
Drug use
Drug treatment
Drug-control legislation
Prescription drugs
The war on drugs
Decriminalization
Legalization
Gambling
Sex work

News Flash #1

Title

News Flash #2

Title

What Agency Am I?
Peruse the following descriptions taken from the websites of federal criminal justice-related agencies, programs, and bureaus. Find the organization that matches it in the list and write it in the blank space provided. Hint: Use the web addresses in the list to check the organizations' websites.

A. I am a law enforcement organization within the United States Department of Justice that enforces the federal laws and regulations relating to alcohol, tobacco, firearms, explosives, and arson. My tasks include ensuring fair and proper revenue collection and supporting federal, state, local, and international law enforcement.

Who Am I? _____

B. My mission is to enforce the controlled substances laws and regulations of the United States and bring to the criminal and civil justice system of the United States, or any other competent jurisdiction, those organizations and principal members of organizations involved in the growing, manufacture, or distribution of controlled substances appearing in or destined for illicit traffic in the United States.

Who Am I? _____

C. I collected nearly $2 trillion in revenue and processed more than 222 million tax returns in 2003. My criminal investigation division investigates potential criminal violations of the Internal Revenue Code and related financial crimes.

Who Am I? _____

D. I am a component of the Executive Office of the President that establishes policies, priorities, and objectives for the nation's drug control program. My goals are to reduce illicit drug use, manufacturing, and trafficking; drug-related crime and violence; and drug-related health consequences. My director produces the National Drug Control Strategy, which directs the nation's anti-drug efforts and establishes a program, budget, and guidelines for cooperation among federal, state, and local entities.

Who Am I? _____

List

Bureau of Alcohol, Tobacco, Firearms and Explosives	http://www.atf.gov
Community Oriented Policing Services	http://www.cops.usdoj.gov
Drug Enforcement Administration	http://www.dea.gov
Federal Judicial Center	http://www.fjc.gov
Internal Revenue Service	http://www.irs.gov
Office of National Drug Control Policy	http://www.whitehousedrugpolicy.gov
U.S. Sentencing Commission	http://www.ussc.gov

Word Search

Instructions: Fill in the blanks of the definitions below with the correct word, then find the word in the puzzle!

```
V J X R R Z H T M F V B E M L B F X N U F P J S B Z F X P R
M X E S U J P I C B Q X P V V E Z N J L V O P A C T X I B B
X V X T Y K U R Q U P S P I G P G F K Q U R G T L Z F V N I
F H U F E F S U E U R F C H I P G A V Z K N E E W D O F C E
S G Y F C D P O C Z G T Y U U D G L L D R O W U H Q K S J P
N O V M I H A J F U I Y V R S G J S P I G G N B I Y N F G Y
D J R O R Y K A T M A C U Q E O E J J L Z R S I S W Q V C I
N V C N H N F M L T B R X T B J M C K C E A X R K X U D N W
X E T Z S T S E B Q R A Q H C R C C U S M P T N E H V U Z D
K I C V X X S Y I V A F N W Y O M Y P A Q H X I Y Q B D L Z
C S U B W S U Y R M M C K A L I E H U A S Y H T O F I Q H N
E P H H I Y Y K Y I W U L I U M Z N Z E C G I G V N H U H O
I V B F S B O C X D B Y G Z P J M P G G O A N F V V Y T K I
S Y O M C O P A K Y A F P L G P I X B Z M M E E M H O O J T
U L X L C G Y J T B G W K Y A R O R G H A B F I W C C U M A
P V S E S U J I K S J M V L L L G N A T M L T T L H O Y G Z
S R Y G R T N N K R O R K Y W D S D S M E I V L G V T C Q I
V W G I I E E Y Z S O R E K L Q V H X M H N J M O V S M L L
C V P D C V C A X D F W S E V T U N U T O G C F R V A V A A
B C P S P C Z N D N R T X M B Y P I C O V A K F Y U L S H N
O R B F Z Y P P Z E R A K E K Y P Y B M W E E L I E W A W I
J O N O R O U R X X G H Q S S O T C U U P Z X Q M S G A Q M
W P W I D T M U B J A B K O B I Y C U N O W E A X E X Z M I
C C Q H K M K Q G Z O S N B N J X C W R N O F R I O Z E T R
C Y B G I U D K U Q X D L U N N P U X O D J K H R O J V U C
G G E Z A N Y I K Z V U M P R O S T I T U T I O N W P P P E
D R I N I P N F A J I M F G E Q L C F V E K P V J N L D I D
C L K O Y I E U I S O H G N U Z U K I L D H C G I P Y C O P
J J Q O S Z P Q X C W K L P I L T L V C P K J Q O V F T X U
P H K N G W E T M F A Y B B F R H I S Z Q M N P G L V X K T
```

Definitions

1. _____ are practices, acts, and/or media accepted by a given social group that shares a geographic area and/or government.

2. The emendation of laws or statutes to lessen or remove penalties for specific acts subject to criminal prosecution, arrest, and imprisonment is called _____.

3. _____ is legal in some form, such as lotteries or casinos, in most states.

4. _____ is the total removal of legal prohibitions on specific acts that were previously proscribed and punishable by law.

5. The 1951 Boggs Act regulated both narcotics and _____ in a single federal law.

6. In *Jacobellis v. Ohio* (1964), Justice Potter Stewart defined _____ by saying, "I know it when I see it."

211

7. During the Civil War, morphine, a highly addictive _____ extract, was widely used to combat pain and dysentery.

8. The tension that exists in the policing of _____ derives from the difference between erotica and obscenity.

9. _____ is illegal in just about every jurisdiction in the United States, with the most well-known exception being state-licensed brothels in Nevada.

10. _____ describes the exchange of coital or sex-related activities for payment.

11. Behaviors that are deemed undesirable because they offend community standards rather than directly harm people or property are called _____.

12. The National Prohibition Act was also known as the _____.

13. The _____ came about in 1791 when Congress passed an excise tax on a certain liquor.

Chapter 16
Present and Emerging Trends: The Future of Criminal Justice

Learning Objectives
After reading this chapter, you should be able to:

1. Discuss the significance of the war metaphor when it is applied to crime.
2. Compare and contrast the war on terrorism with the war on crime.
3. Discuss how terrorism has affected Americans' perception of civil rights.
4. Discuss the Patriot Act.
5. Discuss the Department of Homeland Security and its relationship to the criminal justice system.
6. Compare and contrast peacemaking criminology to the war metaphor for dealing with crime.
7. Discuss restorative justice and its relationship to peacemaking criminology.
8. Describe the peacemaking pyramid.
9. Discuss the principles of restorative justice.
10. Discuss why you may or may not want to pursue a career in criminal justice.

Chapter Summary and Key Concepts
Chapter 16 reviews the war on terrorism, as well as two trends in the criminal justice system: the war on crime and peacemaking.

The War on Terrorism
- Prior to the war on terrorism, the military and law enforcement had different goals and different targets.
- U.S. government agencies that comprise national defense and the criminal justice system are merging in terms of mission, legal authority, and resources.
- Congress created the Department of Homeland Security after September 11, 2001, as a cabinet-level agency with oversight for protecting the United States.
- The Department of Homeland Security comprises several federal law enforcement agencies, including the Secret Service, but not the FBI or the CIA.
- Differences between the war on terrorism and other social problems are that the war on terrorism has a clear and identifiable outside enemy, is political rather than social, and utilizes military weapons. Also, terrorists firmly believe their cause is just, and foreign terrorists do not have U.S. legal protections.
- The Patriot Act is officially titled "Uniting and Strengthening America by Providing Appropriate Tools Required to Intercept and Obstruct Terrorism Act."
- Two components of the Patriot Act that are of particular concern to criminal justice students are the reorganization and re-tasking of federal law enforcement and the implications for civil liberties and legal rights.
- The Patriot Act greatly expands the government's authority to gather information. Controversial aspects of the act include judicial review and secret searches.

- The war on terrorism has affected local criminal justice systems by assigning new responsibilities (unfunded mandates) and increasing the capabilities of local law enforcement with an influx of personnel and equipment (increased capacity).

The War on Crime and Peacemaking
- The criminal justice system may be considered to be struggling between the extremes of waging war on criminals and making peace with citizens.
- The Bill of Rights and legal precedent greatly limit what the criminal justice system can do in pursuit of offenders.
- The Constitution has provisions to protect citizens from an overzealous criminal justice system.
- Critics contend that the war-on-crime approach has made the criminal justice system too punitive and less rehabilitative.
- An alternative to the war metaphor is the peacemaking approach.
- Harold Pepinsky and Richard Quinney envision peacemaking criminology as developing from three intellectual traditions: religious and humanist, feminist, and critical.
- The peacemaking perspective is applicable to four levels of analysis: intrapersonal, interpersonal, societal and institutional, and international and global.
- The peacemaking pyramid includes nonviolence, social justice, inclusion, correct means, ascertainable criteria, and categorical imperative.
- Restorative justice practices involve the community. Programs include victim-offender reconciliation programs, family group conferencing, and victim-offender panels.
- Restorative justice programs seek to make offenders accountable to victims, the community, and themselves.

Key Terms

ascertainable criteria
Peacemaking criminology term that states that everyone involved in a criminal justice process should understand the rules and procedures employed by the system.

categorical imperative
A term associated with the philosopher Immanuel Kant. When applied to peacemaking, it means that every decision should be logical enough to be applied to other cases at other times.

correct means
Peacemaking criminology term coined by Gandhi. A good solution to the problems of crime can only be attained by processes that embody peacemaking principles.

peacemaking criminology
A theoretical perspective that serves as an alternative to the war on crime. It focuses on nonviolence, social justice, and reducing the suffering of both the victim and the offender.

restorative justice
An alternative justice model that uses community programs to repair the harm done by crime. Programs include the victim, the offender, representatives of law enforcement, and representatives of the community in attempting to craft long-lasting and satisfying solutions to the problems of crime.

Short Answer Questions

We have a war on crime, a war on drugs, and now a war on terrorism. Is the war metaphor an appropriate way to think about these problems? What dangers do we risk when we wage a war on our own citizens?

___

___

___

___

___

___

___

___

Describe how the terrorist events of September 11, 2001, have affected the workings of the criminal justice system. Are these changes permanent or will they fade away if there are no further terrorist attacks?

___

___

___

___

___

___

___

Describe the development of peacemaking criminology. What are the major principles of this approach, and who are the major theorists?

How does the restorative justice movement differ from the traditional criminal justice system? Is there any reason to think that restorative justice will be any more successful than traditional criminal justice?

What is the future of the criminal justice system? Will the war on crime perspective continue to receive the most attention or will the peacemaking perspective gain a legitimate and popular standing in the way justice is dispensed in the United States?

___

Study Guide Questions

Multiple Choice

1. Two components of the Patriot Act are of particular concern to the criminal justice student.
   a. federal law enforcement reorganization; issues of civil rights and liberties
   b. federal law enforcement reorganization; the act's sunset clause
   c. issues of civil rights and liberties; weapons for local police
   d. the act's sunset clause; weapons for local police

2. This is at the top of the peacemaking pyramid.
   a. categorical imperative
   b. correct means
   c. ascertainable criteria
   d. nonviolence

3. This means that everyone involved in the criminal justice process should clearly understand how it works.
   a. categorical imperative
   b. ascertainable criteria
   c. correct means
   d. ultimate comprehension

4. According to this ideal postulated by Kant, people should "Act only according to the maxim whereby you can at the same time will that it should become a universal law."
a. correct means
b. universal imperative
c. nonviolence
d. categorical imperative

5. According to Gandhi, crime problems can only be solved satisfactorily by processes that embody peacemaking principles. This philosophy is called
a. zero tolerance.
b. nonviolence.
c. correct means.
d. categorical imperative.

6. The official title of the Patriot Act is
a. the Protecting America by Funding the Department of Homeland Security Act.
b. the War on Terrorism Act.
c. the Patriot Act.
d. the Uniting and Strengthening America by Providing Appropriate Tools Required to Intercept and Obstruct Terrorism Act.

7. These may be used when a victim wishes to address offenders who have committed the type of crime the victim has suffered.
a. victim-offender panels
b. victim-offender reconciliation programs
c. mediation programs
d. family group conferencing

8. After September 11, 2001, several agencies were re-organized into this agency.
a. Department of Justice
b. Department of Homeland Security
c. Treasury Department
d. War Department

9. Which is not part of the Department of Homeland Security?
a. Plum Island Animal Disease Center
b. U.S. Customs and Border Protection
c. U.S. Coast Guard
d. Central Intelligence Agency

10. These two acts limit the government's ability to conduct domestic surveillance.
a. Foreign Intelligence Surveillance Act of 1978; Patriot Act
b. Crime Control and Safe Streets Act of 1968; Patriot Act
c. Crime Control and Safe Streets Act of 1968; Foreign Intelligence Surveillance Act of 1978
d. Crime Control and Safe Streets Act of 1968; Harrison Act

True/False

1. The Constitution allows using the military to deal with routine, domestic crime. _____

2. There are no controversial aspects of the Patriot Act. _____

3. The influence of social characteristics on the justice process is a particularly pressing concern of critical criminologists. _____

4. Restorative justice practices involve the community. _____

5. The war on terrorism is much like the war on drugs. _____

6. Peacemaking criminology is unconcerned with social justice. _____

7. The "war" approach to crime considers criminals the enemy. _____

8. The FBI was left out of the Department of Homeland Security. _____

9. Peacemaking criminology argues that the criminal justice system should heed what the military can offer to law enforcement. _____

10. The war on terrorism has greatly affected local law enforcement. _____

Fill in the Blank

1. _____ is at the base of the peacemaking pyramid.

2. _____ uses a trained mediator to work with the victim and the offender.

3. The principle of _____ suggests that everyone involved in a crime, including its harm and resolution, work together to craft a sentence that fully resolves the dispute.

4. The _____ has provisions to protect citizens from an overzealous criminal justice system.

5. The _____ movement represents the practical application of peacemaking criminology.

6. The peacemaking perspective is applicable to four levels of analysis: _____, _____, _____, and _____.

7. For the most part, the war on _____ and the war on _____ lack a clear, identifiable external enemy.

8. Two of the more controversial aspects of the Patriot Act are _____ and _____.

9. The wars on crime and drugs will be both hindered and aided by the war on terrorism though _____ and _____.

10. _____ uses a mediator to enable all those connected to a crime, including members of the families and community, to work together to develop a solution.

Find a Flash
Read the two news flashes in Chapter 16 carefully, noting how they illustrate issues covered in the chapter.

- *No Atheists in This Prison* describes a "faith-based" prison in Florida.
- *Forgiveness* looks at the use of peacemaking and restorative justice principles in an extreme real-world situation.

Use the library or search the web to find two news items that exemplify, explain, or even appear to contradict topics from Chapter 16. Write short summaries of these news items in the spaces provided. If possible, find one local story and one national story. Give your news flashes short titles that explain what they are about. Suggested news flash topics are listed below.

The war on crime
The war on drugs
The war on terrorism
September 11, 2001
The Patriot Act
Restorative justice

News Flash #1

Title

News Flash #2

Title

What Agency Am I?

Peruse the following descriptions taken from the websites of federal criminal justice-related agencies, programs, and bureaus. Find the organization that matches it in the list and write it in the blank space provided. Hint: Use the web addresses in the list to check the organizations' websites.

A. I enforce federal statutes prohibiting discrimination on the basis of race, sex, handicap, religion, and national origin. I enforce laws that prohibit discrimination in education, employment, credit, housing, public accommodations and facilities, voting, and certain federally funded and conducted programs. In addition, I prosecute actions under several criminal civil rights statutes that preserve personal liberties and safety.

Who Am I? _____

B. Created as a result of the Violent Crime Control and Law Enforcement Act of 1994, I advance community policing in jurisdictions across the country. I provide grants to tribal, state, and local law enforcement agencies to hire and train community-policing professionals; acquire and deploy cutting-edge crime-fighting technologies; and develop and test innovative policing strategies.

Who Am I? _____

C. Established by the 1984 Victims of Crime Act to oversee diverse programs that benefit victims of crime, I provide funding to state victim assistance and compensation programs. I support training designed to educate criminal justice and allied professionals regarding the rights and needs of crime victims.

Who Am I? _____

D. I handle the Justice Department's legal and policy issues regarding violence against women. I work closely with components of other federal agencies to implement the mandates of the Violence Against Women Act and subsequent legislation.

Who Am I? _____

List

Community Oriented Policing Services	http://www.cops.usdoj.gov
Department of Justice Civil Rights Division	http://www.usdoj.gov/crt
Drug Enforcement Administration	http://www.dea.gov
Office for Victims of Crime	http://www.ojp.usdoj.gov/ovc
Office of National Drug Control Policy	http://www.whitehousedrugpolicy.gov
Office on Violence Against Women	http://www.ojp.usdoj.gov/vawo
U.S. Sentencing Commission	http://www.ussc.gov

Word Search

Instructions: Fill in the blanks of the definitions below with the correct word, then find the word in the puzzle!

```
N Z A X F H C N Q W K G C Y U N X V D I O N X J C J J J Y M
N V J O S I J C F N Y U D X S W T M Z T U Y E Z K W J Y S R
O B A A R R L R K G S R T B Z P H R I W S D X K H O J R F Y
N N U Y U G N I K A M E C A E P M S T E S R O T R Y Y W Q O
V H X W L V I E F T F U D M Z W A Z U W T B W C N U A N I L
I U U Y O W L K G Q T H P Q F P S K L Y B D Z R X K J J K S
O X S O P H U B O W K W W C D X C M T Z O L H Q Z U O K M K
L B Z P V Z J I B L G M O E K K B H Y D M T K I W T N W Q F
E N Q O U D Q O W M I R E S J W Z F U H K Q Q B T Q E Y J I
N N R U C B N I Q N R V X C X F R A L O B L Q W Y O G I U H
C W U Q I S U W L E I R Q U E Z U L J O C A G R L T N C G C
E N V Y A U O L C T P N E Z W I O D F S L P Z G T C Z S Y R
S Y B V H X D T A Y N B G T A U J Z L X I M J V L E W O Q C
F B H T F C M R A O L F E S J J O W M S I K A U E G B V T Y
I O R K Z E O W B J J N F O P G Z L M W L Z S H I A Y L T O
O N Y Q A T H A D J C C F C B S Z Z W U W I Q W S C L A C B
D G M N S N J E X C R L B I Q C F U P J O C U C P D P U A W
K W S E H Y X R U G N E L A T Q B G B N L N E H M B P F T A
Z X R Y U Y M A K A O N W L Q K A L C C V R O P Z U F G O J
Z T N N L J H U M P I V N J Z N P R G A T N Z C G F N Y I P
Y G X C C B G V I G J F Y U G O S M M A L S H A T O Y E R G
D R B W M M Q E Y Z F I Q S U T F L I S N N S E H T U Z T G
J U O K U X G T U F A Q W T F I R N I W I V L X A N A A A M
M M X L P A T E R R O R N I V T A U D W T J W P R F Y Z P D
J W H C D F Z L M K E B J C F B U N R L I K U D Z Q W S A Z
Y G N Y X A T M J P M I D E L H Q U S A U Z S Q D O F W B U
H V U Y H W T X B Q X R P E S C U D W X D K M X H Y D X X P
G R N W M C H J O U A M F R S B W F T V V H F F H M P Z W F
H B C W U B J O H H Y X Z F H V A G C Z F R F A D S Y I W B
N C H O Z A V O J M Z Y Q M R W D O F B Y A T A D G R D F G
```

Definitions

1. The official title of the _____ is "Uniting and Strengthening America by Providing Appropriate Tools Required to Intercept and Obstruct Terrorism Act."

2. In many ways, the war on _____ is different than the war on crime or the war on drugs.

3. One alternative to the war metaphor is the _____ approach.

4. According to the principles of _____ justice, the criminal justice system is just a small part of society's response to crime.

5. The six steps of the Peacemaking Pyramid are: _____ criteria, _____, _____, _____, _____, and _____.

Match the Case

Part Five
Problems in the Crosscurrents

Draw a line from the case to its outcome.

Schall v. Martin   The distribution of marijuana, even for medical purposes and with approval by a state's citizens, is prohibited under the Controlled Substances Act.

Miller v. California   The U.S. Supreme Court ruled that a juvenile's due process rights are denied when his or her case is waived to adult criminal court without a formal hearing.

In re Gault   This Nevada Supreme Court case demonstrates the continuing debate over the legalization of sex work in the only state where sex work is legal.

Kent v. United States   Juveniles' right to an attorney, as well the right to confront accusers and protection from self-incrimination, is established.

Nye County v. Plankinton   If incarceration or loss of freedom is possible, a case against a juvenile must be proved beyond a reasonable doubt.

In re Winship   The U.S. Supreme Court set forth a new three-part test for obscenity.

United States v. Oakland Cannabis   As long as procedures protect a juvenile's rights, detention of a juvenile is constitutional if it protects the juvenile and society from crimes he or she may commit pre-trial.

Appendix A

Answers to Even-Numbered Study Guide Questions

Chapter 1		
Multiple Choice	True/False	Fill in the Blank
2. c	2. F	2. Grand jury
4. d	4. T	4. goals
6. a	6. F	6. Uniform Crime Reports (UCR)
8. a	8. T	8. criminal justice system
10. c	10. F	10. jail
Chapter 2		
Multiple Choice	True/False	Fill in the Blank
2. d	2. T	2. jurisdictions
4. d	4. F	4. property
6. d	6. T	6. person
8. b	8. T	8. self-report study (or victimization study); Uniform Crime Reports (or National Incident-Based Reporting System)
10. b	10. T	10. Victim precipitation
Chapter 3		
Multiple Choice	True/False	Fill in the Blank
2. c	2. F	2. behaviorism
4. b	4. F	4. anomie
6. a	6. T	6. utilitarianism
8. c	8. T	8. socialist feminist criminology
10 b	10. T	10. Sigmund Freud
Chapter 4		
Multiple Choice	True/False	Fill in the Blank
2. b	2. F	2. jurisdiction
4. c	4. T	4. amendments
6. a	6. T	6. inchoate
8. a	8. F	8. concurrence
10. d	10. F	10. Magna Carta
Chapter 5		
Multiple Choice	True/False	Fill in the Blank
2. d	2. F	2. due process rights
4. b	4. F	4. Orlando W. Wilson
6. c	6. T	6. Secret Service
8. a	8. T	8. Department of the Treasury
10. c	10. T	10. J. Edgar Hoover

Chapter 6		
Multiple Choice	True/False	Fill in the Blank
2. d	2. F	2. policeman's working personality
4. b	4. F	4. discretion
6. a	6. T	6. unreasonable
8. c	8. F	8. *Terry v. Ohio*
10. c	10. T	10. watchman

Chapter 7		
Multiple Choice	True/False	Fill in the Blank
2. c	2. T	2. Neighborhood watch
4. d	4. T	4. *Tennessee v. Garner*
6. a	6. T	6. force
8. d	8. F	8. hierarchical
10. b	10. T	10. danger; isolation; authority; suspicion

Chapter 8		
Multiple Choice	True/False	Fill in the Blank
2. a	2. T	2. *McCulloch v. Maryland*
4. d	4. F	4. Jurisdiction
6. d	6. T	6. *Marbury v. Madison*
8. b	8. F	8. magistrate; district; Appeal
10. b	10. T	10. inquest

Chapter 9		
Multiple Choice	True/False	Fill in the Blank
2. a	2. F	2. *United States v. Leon*
4. a	4. T	4. disposition
6. d	6. F	6. judge
8. b	8. F	8. Executive selection
10. a	10. F	10. Criminal Division

Chapter 10		
Multiple Choice	True/False	Fill in the Blank
2. d	2. F	2. master jury list
4. b	4. T	4. direct
6. a	6. F	6. cross-examine
8. c	8. T	8. *U.S. v. Salerno*
10. d	10. F	10. presumptive sentence

Chapter 11		
Multiple Choice	True/False	Fill in the Blank
2. b	2. T	2. Zebulon Brockway
4. a	4. F	4. Auburn
6. b	6. T	6. retributive
8. d	8. F	8. incarceration
10. b	10. F	10. Eastern State

Chapter 12		
Multiple Choice	True/False	Fill in the Blank
2. a	2. T	2. Fourteenth
4. d	4. F	4. Pelican Bay
6. c	6. F	6. executive
8. d	8. F	8. *Wolff v. McDonnell*
10. a	10. F	10. private

Chapter 13		
Multiple Choice	True/False	Fill in the Blank
2. c	2. F	2. shock probation
4. a	4. T	4. Jails
6. b	6. T	6. prison
8. d	8. T	8. intensive supervision probation
10. b	10. T	10. pre-sentence investigation

Chapter 14		
Multiple Choice	True/False	Fill in the Blank
2. d	2. T	2. Zero-tolerance
4. d	4. T	4. petitioner
6. c	6. F	6. adversarial
8. a	8. T	8. attorney; self-incrimination
10. b	10. F	10. Illinois

Chapter 15		
Multiple Choice	True/False	Fill in the Blank
2. d	2. F	2. morphine
4. a	4. F	4. call girl; male escort
6. c	6. T	6. *Nye County v. Plankinton*
8. d	8. F	8. Narcotics Control Act
10. c	10. F	10. decriminalization

Chapter 16		
Multiple Choice	True/False	Fill in the Blank
2. a	2. F	2. victim-offender reconciliation program
4. d	4. T	4. Constitution
6. d	6. F	6. intrapersonal; interpersonal; societal and institutional; international and global
8. b	8. T	8. judicial review; secret searches
10. c	10. T	10. Family group conferencing